Vocal Health for Singers

A Leading Voice Doctor Answers over 100 Questions from Vocalists

Anthony F. Jahn

MD, FACS, FRCS(C)

ISBN: 978-0-9920344-4-3

Praise for
Vocal Health for Singers

"Regarded as one of America's top voice doctors specializing in singers, Dr. Anthony Jahn tackles the most common questions and concerns, providing simple answers and clear directions. In this tiny book, you'll learn a ton about proper water intake, mucus control and how to protect yourself against common ailments which plague all singers. And some of Dr. Jahn's answers may surprise you!"

-Lisa Popeil, Top LA Vocal Coach, creator of Voiceworks®

"As a vocal coach, singer, and most importantly, the guy who shatters glass with his voice for a living, vocal health is of utmost important to me. It is a rare to find a doctor who understands the needs of the voice professional, and is open to both medical and natural ways of healing, protecting, and aiding the singer/speaker. Which is why I was pleased to read Dr. Anthony F. Jahn's book. While approaching the voice from the medical professional's view, he has offered great advice on how to care for the voice with simple solutions that will not sacrifice the voice in the long run. This is great guide to keep in your gig bag!"

-Jaime Vendera, vocal coach renowned for his wineglass-shattering voice

"This valuable writing by Tony Jahn is a welcome addition to the wide variety of books intended to enrich singers' knowledge in regard to their precious musical instrument: the vocal folds and tract. This concise and practical volume is rich with advice, facts and knowledge – all important materials for a long and healthy vocal career within a highly demanding occupation – presented in an easily digestible form by one of the masters in this field."

-Moshe Harell, MD, Otolaryngologist and Professional Voice specialist, Israel

"Few doctors know the needs of a singers as well as Tony Jahn. With his knowledge and skills he has helped and rescued known and unknown singers in times of medical trouble. This book reflects his expertise and his emphatic personality."

-Marco Franken MD, laryngologist, Consultant Royal Conservatory - The Hague, Netherlands

"This is a practical source of valuable information for professional singers and actors which debunks the myths and misconceptions regarding proper care of the voice - and sets the record straight. Dr. Anthony Jahn uses a sagacious blend of uncomplicated scientific explanation with a common sense approach, making his counsel easy to trust and easy to use. A must have for singers and actors at any level, beginner or professional."

-Ron Browning, International Voice Coach to the Stars

Preface

This little book began years ago as a series of questions sent by singers dealing with common medical problems. While some of these issues might seem trivial to those whose livelihood does not depend on their voice, for vocalists they are serious, career-impacting concerns that deserve the doctor's attention and considered advice. I hope you will be able to use the information here to the benefit of your voice, your health, and your livelihood.

Many of these questions were first published in Classical Singer magazine and on the VoiceCouncil Magazine website. Some have been rewritten, and we have also included several new pieces that have not been previously available.

My thanks to Gregory A. Barker, Commissioning Editor at VoiceCouncil.com, for his expert assistance, as well as to Sara Thomas (Editor) and David Wood (Publisher) of Classical Singer Magazine for their generosity and support.

As a final note, please consider that while you may find useful information here, the answers here are just guidelines, and should not be considered as specific medical advice. Nothing takes the place of a private medical consultation, and if you have medical problems, you should attend to them with your own physician.

My best wishes for good health and a long and successful career.

-Anthony F. Jahn, MD

Contents

1. Get the Basics Right

How Important is Water for a Healthy, Working Voice? **13**

The Benefits of Sipping and Swallowing During Gigs **14**

When to Drink Water and Why **16**

Does Coffee Really Dry Out the Voice? **17**

Too Much Mucus? **18**

Make Friends with Your Mucus **20**

Why is Phlegm Ruining My Student's Range? **21**

How Can I Stop Constant Throat Clearing? **23**

2. Prevail over Colds and Flu

How Can I Defend Myself from Winter Germs? **24**

The Perils and Precautions of Singing with a Cold **25**

I HAVE to Sing with an Infection – What Can I Do? **27**

Rhinitis is Ruining my Range! **29**

Can Constant Illness Damage My Voice Forever? **30**

How Soon Will My Voice Return After Illness? **31**

What's the Safest Way to Clear My Throat? **33**

Seeking a Magical Cure for My Throat Infection **34**

Have Throat Germs Travelled Down to my Voice? **35**

How to Treat Freshman's Flu **36**

How Can I Cure my Lengthy Laryngitis? **37**

How Can I Deal with Marathon Colds? **38**

3. Perfect Vocal Care

Do I Really Need to Take Care of My Voice? **39**

What is Vocal Rest and When Should I Do it? **40**

How Can I Get a Voice Doctor Appointment? **42**

Saline Nasal Flushing Feels like Drowning! **43**

Meditation Chanting: Good or Bad for my Voice? **44**

Vocal Weakness After Illness – What's Going On? **45**

The Side Effects of Cigarettes **46**

How Do I Un-Wax my Ears? **48**

There are Gigs in the Diary and My Voice is Raspy! **49**

Need Speedy Recovery After Demanding Gig! **50**

How Can I Sober Up my Voice? **51**

Why Is There So Much "Air" In My Tone? **52**

4. Keep Your Energy Up!

Can I Energize my Old Tired Voice? **53**

Is Brandy OK as Part of my Pre-Gig Warm up? **54**

How Sick Does a Singer Have to be to Stop Singing? **55**

Can a Vegetarian Rock the Stage? **56**

Should I be a Vocal Athlete? **57**

Exhaustion Affecting Singing Stamina **58**

Can I Swim Then Sing? **60**

Am I Running my Voice into the Ground? **61**

Singing Makes me Dizzy! **62**

Will Drastic Dieting Starve my Voice? **63**

Can I Sing Well with a Hernia? **64**

The Connection Between Thyroid Disease and Singing **65**

Singing with an Eating Disorder **66**

Why is Swimming Exhausting my Voice? **67**

How Do I Stamp out Sleep Apnea? **68**

5. Get a Gig Ready Voice

Can I Wake Up with a Gig-Ready Voice? **70**

Am I Losing My Upper Range? **71**

Is it Normal to Feel Pain After Singing? **73**

Can Talking Well Improve My Singing? **74**

How Can I Kickstart my Morning Voice? **76**

How Can I Make a Sexy Breathy Sound? **78**

How Can I Make My Morning Voice Remain? **80**

My Voice is Getting Old – Can I Wind Back the Clock? **81**

Can I Body-Build my Voice Muscles? **83**

What Do the False Folds Do? **86**

What Should my Tongue Be Doing When I'm Singing? **87**

Can You Solve My Mysterious Throat Pain? **89**

What's Happening Inside My Breathy Tone? **90**

At What Age is a Voice Fully Grown? **91**

How Can I Get Rid of Habitual Jaw Tension? **92**

6. Travel in Style

How Can I Have a Healthy Tour? **94**

I'm Going Mad with a Blocked Ear! **96**

Can I Shield my Voice from a Smoky Environment? **97**

The Nevada Desert is Drying Out my Voice! **99**

How Can I Find Vocal Power on Tour? **100**

How Can I Cure Blocked Ears When Flying? **101**

What's The Best Way to Medicate Travel Sickness? **103**

Flying Without Mucus **104**

7. To Medicate or Not Medicate?

What's the Truth About Menthol Lozenges? **105**

No Medication Can Beat my Phlegm! **106**

Hemorrhoid Cream for the Voice – Cure or Quackery? **107**

Will Attention Deficit Disorder Meds Rattle my Voice? **108**

Do Nasal Sprays Have Long Term Side Effects? **109**

What Are The Downsides of Anti-Depressants? **111**

What is the Best Acne Treatment? **112**

Will A Steroid Nasal Spray Make My Voice Raspy? **113**

8. Master Reflux for Good

How Does Stomach Acid Reach the Voice? **114**

What are the Side Effects to Reflux Medication? **115**

Is it Possible to be Addicted to Reflux Treatment? **116**

Are Antibiotics Giving Me Reflux? **117**

Can You Help My Problem with Swallowing? **118**

Can Coffee Cause Reflux? **119**

Are My Wisdom Teeth Causing Vocal Trouble? **120**

Does Reflux Make my Throat Tight? **121**

Can Reflux Cause Oral Yeast Infections? **122**

Are Antihistamines and Reflux Linked? **123**

9. Women's Corner

Does Menstruation Make Me Sing Badly? **125**

Best Way to Deal with Gynaecological Issues? **126**

When is a Woman's Voice Finished Growing? **128**

Do Thyroid Medications Affect Singing? **129**

Will Hormones Cause Permanent Damage to my Voice? **129**

Can I Find My Pre-Pregnancy Voice? **130**

Will the Pill Deepen my Voice? **131**

Is Breastfeeding Tightening my Voice? **132**

Can I Regain my Pre-Birth Control Range? **133**

Will Pregnancy Hormones Wreck My Voice? **134**

Will the Pill Bring Back my Low Notes? **135**

Is PMS Making my Voice Breathy? **136**

I'm Clueless About Hormone Replacement Therapy **137**

10. Before and After Surgery

How Can I Recover from Nodules? **138**

Is it Nodules or a Polyp? **140**

What Vocal Rest Do I need After Laryngeal Surgery? **141**

Will a Nose Job Change my Voice? **143**

Should I have my Snoring Tonsils Removed? **144**

I'm Scared to Have Sleep Apnea Surgery! **145**

Is it Wise to Remove Wisdom Teeth? **146**

How Do I Gain my Pre-Op Breathing Power? **147**

Tonsil Scarring is Dampening my Voice **148**

My Post-Op Voice Feels Strange **149**

Can Tonsils Cause Hoarseness? **150**

Can Tonsils Cause Trouble for the Voice? **151**

Can Wind Instruments Cause Nodules? **152**

Will a Tummy Tuck Decrease my Vocal Power? **153**

11. Dealing with Asthma and Allergies

Can Asthma Treatment Ruin my Singing? **155**

Asthma Symptoms Are Holding Me Back **156**

Would an Asthma Inhaler Make the Voice Feel Sluggish? **157**

Is my Asthma Inhaler Cracking my High Notes? **158**

Symptom-Free Asthma Treatment: Myth or Reality? **160**

Seeking Moisture in a Dry Environment **161**

Seeking Solutions for Seasonal Voice Loss **163**

Am I Allergic to my New Neighborhood? **164**

How Do I Maintain Vocal Health Around Wildfires? **165**

12. Stage Fright and Vocal Health

My Stage Fright Causes Emergency Toilet Trips! **167**

Will my Worrying Jinx my Vocal Health? **168**

My Band Won't Change Song Keys – What Can I do? **170**

Could Stage Fright Medication Mess with my Voice? **171**

My Stage Fright is Ruining my Career! **172**

Help Me Battle My Fear of Dentists! **173**

Could Braces Clamp Up my Voice? **174**

How Do You Sing with Hearing Aids? **175**

1. Get the Basics Right

How Important is Water for a Healthy, Working Voice?

Dear Doctor Jahn,

Would you say that water is the closest thing we have to a "cure-all" when it comes to singing? I mean, I do a lot of singing in bars and clubs and I drink a LOT of water and I really haven't had issues that other questioners have (hoarseness, sore-throats etc.) - Gus

Dear Gus,

Since our bodies are mostly water, it would make sense that staying wet will allow our bodies to function optimally. I normally recommend eight 8 oz. glasses of water a day, but this should be increased if you are exercising and perspiring.

Water is the common currency of our cells, both inside and out, and it is the main vehicle for our circulation; it allows for the exchange of nutrients and the elimination of wastes. Specifically, from the singer's point of view, the vocal folds need to be both hydrated from the inside, and lubricated on their surface. Surface lubrication comes from glands in the ventricles just above the vocal folds, and requires (surprise!) drinking water.

This allows them to move more easily, approximate more exactly, and, most importantly, it reduces trauma to the mucous membranes.

When you ice skate, your blades actually slide on a very thin layer of water, which is ice that has been melted by the weight of your body pushing down on the skates.

Similarly, when singing, especially in the high range, the vocal folds make contact through a thin film of water. If this layer of water is missing or inadequate due to lack of hydration, the mucous membranes rub against each other, causing inflammation, swelling and possible injury.

The other good thing about drinking so much water during your gigs is that you are drinking less alcohol! Alcohol dehydrates your body and increases the likelihood of trauma to the dried mucous membrane surface.

So, keep drinking water, and sing on!

The Benefits of Sipping and Swallowing During Gigs

Dear Doctor Jahn,

I've heard that the water you drink never actually touches your vocal folds. So why does it feel so good to drink water during my gigs, if the water isn't even coming in contact with them? - Jerry

Dear Jerry,

You're absolutely right: the water you swallow does not touch your vocal folds. Indeed, if it did, you would start to cough and choke, as happens when your drink goes down "the wrong way".

The vocal folds are sensitive to touch and spring into action to protect your trachea and lower airway from anything you might eat or drink.

So where does the water go? Well, there is a lot more to the vocal tract than the vocal folds.

The mouth, the tongue, your pharynx (the back of the throat, which begins behind the nose and extends down to just above the larynx), including all of the structures above and behind the larynx – these all are involved in singing.

From the pharyngeal point of view, singing is little more than muscular effort, vibration, and a constant drying flow of exhaled air rushing past. All of these activities are made easier by lubrication, both of the mucous membrane surfaces (as water rushes by) and internally (as you rehydrate). The cooling and possible increase in humidity in the vocal tract from drinking may further facilitate the vocal effort.

There is yet another aspect to consider, however. When you sing, especially with some strain, you contract one set of muscles, often over a period of time. The act of swallowing activates another set of muscles. During the swallow, the singing muscles get to relax, and even get a bit of passive stretch, which feels good —a bit like relaxing a tightly clenched fist after a minute or two. And here is the most interesting one: swallowing stimulates the vagus nerve, a nerve that has many functions, including slowing the heart rate.

In moments of high effort or excitement, this cardiac effect may feel welcome. Taken all together, the very act of swallowing gives you and your larynx a "breather", a moment of respite before you start to contract the singing muscles again.

When to Drink Water and Why

Dear Doctor Jahn,

Everyone always says "drink water well before your gig" because the water doesn't touch the folds but needs to be absorbed before it can hydrate the voice. But it always feels good to drink water as I'm performing! So I am wondering if this is not the whole truth! Does the immediate effect of the water on the mouth/throat lining above the vocal folds also, in some way, impact the lining on the vocal folds and therefore help my singing immediately? - Kevin

Dear Kevin,

Consider what happens when you perform:

Your mouth is open and you may be sweating, two facts that add to your insensible water loss.

It is somewhat like exercising – you're losing more water and need to replace it. Most importantly, however, the excitement of the performance pumps adrenaline, causing what is called a sympathetic response. Adrenaline shuts off many of the secretory glands, and guess what? Your mouth and throat get dry. So definitely drink, not just before the show for hydration (but don't overload your stomach), but also during the show. All of this is why you report feeling good.

As a general principle, hydration is good. More specifically, as a singer your entire respiratory and vocal tract benefits from drinking water. So as a baseline, I recommend drinking water throughout the day.

It is best to spread this over your day – like "grazing" when you eat. That way, the water is absorbed easily, and you're not overly distending your stomach, which might impair breathing and support. We generally recommend eight 8 oz. glasses a day, two with each meal and one between meals.

Finally, if you think about what happens when you drink during the show, you will realize that it gives you a little break and causes your larynx to move up and down in the neck, almost like a momentary massage to your vocal tract.

So keep sipping! The bottle or glass of water on stage is now a generally accepted prop, and will not interfere with your performance.

Does Coffee Really Dry Out the Voice?

Dear Doctor Jahn,

What is the verdict on caffeine and the voice? I have heard that it doesn't actually dry out the voice that much. Can I start enjoying the odd cup of coffee without hurting my voice? - John

Dear John,

You're right, and as a fellow coffee drinker, I'm pleased to debunk that theory. Drinking coffee (or other caffeinated drinks) does increase the urge to urinate, however.

This is misconstrued by many as evidence that caffeine is a diuretic, therefore drying. I used to believe (and teach) this also, but I have been told by urologist colleagues that this is not the case.

Rather, coffee makes muscles more irritable and contractile. The bladder muscle will therefore signal you to "go" more readily, with smaller degrees of distention. So you may pee twice as frequently, but your urine output is the same.

Now, excessive amounts of caffeine may be a problem – not from dehydration, but because you may lose some neuromuscular control over your voice. This would manifest in singing softly as a tremor.

All said and done, coffee has been shown to have other health benefits, and a daily cup of joe will definitely not hurt your singing.

Too Much Mucus?

Dear Doctor Jahn,

This is going to sound a bit gross, but I have an excess of mucus, so I'm always clearing my throat. It happens throughout the year so I don't think it's from allergies. I also don't eat much in the way of foods like cheese and milk etc. It's really bothersome and, as a result, I don't think I am singing at my best – what can I do? (P.S. I don't like taking strong meds.) - Gary

Dear Gary,

Did you know that a whole book was once written about mucus? Titled "De Catarrhis", it was written by Dr. Schneider in Wittenberg, Germany. The year was 1651, but almost 400 years later, the stuff continues to plague singers.

Mucus is a normal and important lubricant of mucous membranes. It helps to coat and protect (sounds almost like a patriotic motto, doesn't it?) and is also involved in cleaning the surface of the membranes.

We all make and swallow between a pint and a quart of mucus every day. This mucus, a thin and slippery layer, passes through our GI tract silently.

Mucus typically becomes a problem when there is too much, or when it is of the wrong consistency (i.e. too viscous). So to address your problem, you need to consider how to thin the viscous stuff out, and, if excessive, how to get rid of it.

Thinning out mucus requires that you drink lots of water. I recommend eight 8-oz glasses a day. Spread it out over the course of the day, and drink even a bit more if exercising or sweating. Washing it away, in turn, requires irrigating your nose with saline at least twice a day. Showering with plenty of hot steam also helps to loosen the stuff.

You need to also consider why you may be forming excessive (or thick) mucus in the first place. Any sort of inflammation, whether an infection or allergies, can cause excess thick mucus. Consider, also, that even normal mucus will adhere to inflamed surfaces, and then become symptomatic.

For this reason, patients with acid reflux irritation of the pharynx and larynx often complain of the need to clear their throat, and we will even see mucus sticking to the vocal folds when excessive singing has traumatized them.

By way of medical treatment, in addition to hydration and saline irrigation, consider treating reflux and allergies, both by reducing your exposure to irritants and spicy foods, and possibly seeing an allergist or gastroenterologist.

If you decide to self-treat, one caution: beware of antihistamines that are drying and can make your mucus more tenacious. A dry larynx is not only difficult to sing with, but is more prone to injury and vocal nodules.

Make Friends with Your Mucus

Dear Doctor Jahn,

I am being assaulted by phlegm when I perform! I even hate revealing this! But when I get on stage the inner mucus production seems to go into over-drive and I am constantly clearing my throat and swallowing. I want to be free of this! How? - Philippa

Great question, Philippa! There may be a number of reasons, and I have some suggestions for treating this. One thing you DON'T want to do is to load up on drying antihistamines – you won't be able to sing well, particularly the high, quieter passages, and the mucus will thicken. Your larynx needs to be moist and supple, but not coated with mucilage, that's for sure.

Try the following. First, drink lots of water on the day of your performance (you should do this generally, but make a special effort on those days). Look at any medications you may routinely take which cause dryness; common ones are antihistamines, antidepressants and diuretics.

If you have a choice, take these early in the morning or at night - after the show and before going to bed, rather than before singing. Next, clear your nose and upper passages of mucus. We all produce a pint to a quart of mucus a day; you need to clear the stuff out! If you can inhale some steam from a personal facial mask-type steamer, or in a shower, or even from a pan of hot water, that should help. Drip one or two drops of eucalyptus oil into the water.

You can also irrigate your nose with salt water before the show, just to clear out those recalcitrant bits that may be hiding in the back. If you are making more nasal mucus than usual (such as with allergies or a cold), consider using a topical vasoconstrictor such as Afrin or Otrivin nasal spray – this opens your nose but also reduces mucus secretion.

If you are prone to reflux, the acid can irritate the hypopharynx and larynx, making the mucus stickier and adherent to the vocal folds.

Take some antacids to reduce acid reflux. Even if you are not normally prone to reflux, you may get some "agita" before going on stage, so chewing on a Tums before the show may be helpful.

Finally, it is not uncommon nowadays for performers to have a cup of water, cold or hot, sitting on the stool or on the piano while they perform. Intermittent sips will carry the mucus away from your vocal tract and into your stomach where it will not cause you any problems.

Why is Phlegm Ruining My Student's Range?

Dear Doctor Jahn,

I have a student that produces a lot of phlegm (heard as a "gravel-rattle" kind of sound) in his upper range of head voice. He's not unwell (or been unwell) so it's not connected to a virus or bacterial infection. It's quite disconcerting as we've already worked on all the obvious things – trying to cut down on dairy foods, steaming, introducing more water, reducing stress, warming up gently etc. etc. but we haven't seen any real improvement. - Tracey

Yes, phlegm is a chronic issue, Tracey, one that is annoying to non-singers but a major problem for singers. In brief, phlegm is just thickened mucus. Mucus is a secretion that is formed in the upper respiratory tract and normally cleared back from the nose and sinuses into the pharynx and swallowed.

We do this unawares several times a minute, and generally manage to keep the upper aero digestive tract moist and free of any debris. When the mucus becomes excessive or too thick, phlegm forms, and this is not easily cleared, but tends to accumulate and cause problems.

In the larynx, phlegm often collects on the vocal folds at their point of maximal vibration (think of turning a skipping rope with a ring on it - the ring will wind up at the point of maximal excursion).

Since the vocal folds are thinnest, longest, and vibrate most delicately at higher pitches, the clump of mucus becomes most problematic in this range.

Here are some suggestions: first, thin the mucus by drinking about 64 oz (that's eight 8 ounce glasses) of water a day. Next, wash the nose with a Neti pot twice a day to clear out excessive postnasal drip. Next, look at any possible allergies. In addition to inhalant allergies, consider food allergies as well. Apart from dairy and gluten, consider the excessive sugar found in sweets.

Mucus, whether excessive in quantity or consistency, often adheres to areas of irritated mucous membrane. A common cause of inflammation in the laryngeal area is laryngopharyngeal acid reflux, so this needs to be addressed with changes in diet and medical measures to reduce reflux.

Finally, excessive singing - either belting or pushing - can cause irritation of the vocal folds in the area of maximal vibration. This is not nodes or a "pre-nodular condition", simply irritation and mild swelling along the vibrating edge of the vocal fold. Mucus often adheres to this area, something that a laryngologist should be able to see and that you, as a voice teacher (perhaps with input from a vocal therapist), should be able to address.

How Can I Stop Constant Throat Clearing?

Dear Doctor Jahn,

I have a problem where I am always clearing my throat. I always have mucus on my vocal cords. I don't have any allergies that I know of. Any suggestions? - Amy

Dear Amy,

I have several thoughts. Do you drink enough water? You need 8-10 glasses a day (two with each meal, two between each meal), in addition to any coffee, tea or other drinks. Try to avoid milk products for a few weeks. Irrigate your nose twice daily with salt water to reduce any post-nasal drip. Try to avoid drying medications such as antihistamines, antidepressants or decongestants. And finally, if you have any heartburn or gastroesophageal reflux, have it treated.

2. Prevail over Colds and Flu

How Can I Defend Myself from Winter Germs?

Dear Doctor Jahn,

I literally can't afford to catch a cold this time of year! Too many important gigs lined up. So, what are my best chances to avoid catching one – or, if I get one (gasp!), what is my quickest way through it? I'm wondering if you will tell me anything my mother hasn't already... - Kitty

Dear Kitty,

If your mother is like mine it is unlikely I can do better than her, but here it goes.

First, stay healthy: eat and drink enough, get adequate sleep, exercise regularly and avoid stress as much as possible. Stress can weaken your immune system and make you more vulnerable to the cold virus.

Second, minimize the potential for contagion: wash your hands several times a day, especially before touching your face (monitor that you don't touch your face unnecessarily or habitually), don't shake hands with sick people and try to avoid crowded places as much as you can.

At the risk of looking silly, cover your face with a scarf if you need to go on a crowded bus or train during rush hour. If anyone in your family (or a roommate) gets sick, minimize direct physical contact and don't share personal items such as toiletries, dishes or cutlery.

On the active side of prevention, take Vitamin C - about 1000 mg a day in divided doses during cold season. If a cold starts, you can increase this to 4000 mg. Other remedies such as Echinacea may also be helpful, but Vitamin C clearly is beneficial, as long as there are no contra indicatory health issues (such as kidney stones) in your history. Remedies containing Vitamin C, such as Emergen-C or Airborne, are very useful— I don't know if you have them in the U.K., but they are effervescent tablets with vitamins and other remedies that you can drink at the onset of a cold. Once your cold starts, zinc lozenges are very useful, as are zinc nasal swabs — not as a preventive, but they do shorten the cold, making the symptoms less severe and you less contagious. (Avoid zinc nasal spray, since some patients have reported a loss of smell using the spray formulation.)

If you do get sick, stop exercising, stay warm, drink lots of fluids and let your body heal itself. You do not need antibiotics unless the viral cold leads to a secondary bacterial infection, which manifests with mucus that is green or yellow.

The Perils and Precautions of Singing with a Cold

Dear Doctor Jahn,

Is it OK to keep singing even when I've got a cough and sore throat? On the one hand I don't want to become a hypochondriac afraid to push myself, but on the other hand I don't want to do any damage which will affect the gigs I have after I get over my cold. - Kelly

Dear Kelly,

In general, when you have a cold or a sore throat, it is better not to sing. But not everyone has the luxury of cancelling gigs when they get sick; for many reasons - professional, financial, personal - the show may need to go on.

While opera singers often have the stage manager make an announcement before the opera, hoping for a more forgiving and supportive audience, this is not always the custom with popular music. So, if you do need to perform with a cold or a sore throat, first do whatever you can to minimize stress on your throat.

Some suggestions are: reducing the number of songs in the set, eliminating songs that are particularly high and "belty", substituting songs that are more limited in range and dynamic, transposing down (if you have time and opportunity), amplifying more aggressively, and absolutely avoiding social voice use between sets. Once you have adjusted all of these "environmental" factors, treat your specific symptoms aggressively.

For a sore throat, take analgesics (aspirin or ibuprofen) to control the pain. Hot ginger tea is great for a sore throat, and warm saline gargle can also reduce the discomfort. For nasal congestion, take Sudafed (pseudoephedrine); this will decongest and open your passages, and is less drying than antihistamines. I generally recommend staying away from proprietary compounds such as Dayquil, since they often have more ingredients than you need (like a cough suppressant), and tend to be quite drying. A decongestant nasal spray such as Otrivine or Neosynephrine is also useful.

Drink plenty of water throughout the show - just have that water bottle up there beside you on stage. This has now become an accepted convention, so ask for it before you start your performance.

Remember, when you sing with a cold your voice will not sound normal, and how you produce that voice will also be impaired.

Don't try to produce your "normal" voice based on your auditory and proprioceptive (your body's sense of position) memory - your laryngeal agility, resonance and projection will be altered by the infection, and trying to achieve your normal sound may lead to excessive strain on the vocal tract, which may need voice therapy later on to undo.

You will know this is the case if your voice continues to sound abnormal after the infection has cleared, or if you continue to experience throat pain or excessive strain during singing.

I HAVE to Sing with an Infection – What Can I Do?

Dear Doctor Jahn,

When I have a bad cough and sore throat, I know I shouldn't sing, but what if I have a gig I can't get out of? What can I do to minimize harm to my voice? - Steve

Dear Steve,

While there are many potential causes for a sore throat and another bunch of causes for a cough, when the two occur together, you most likely have an infection. The ideal treatment of rest, hydration and not singing may not be an option if you have an important gig.

So, here are some things you can do to minimize harm to yourself. Let me preface this by saying that you should not make performing with an infection a habit: you need to give your body the chance to fight that infection and recover, whenever possible.

You need to do three things: treat the infection, minimize the symptoms, and adjust the parameters of your performance, all with the idea of lessening the impact of the additional strain on your body. Dealing with the infection: if you have a bacterial infection, manifested by a red and swollen throat, tender neck glands and a cough productive of colored sputum, take antibiotics.

Remember to stop drinking alcohol while you are on antibiotics. Additionally, start taking Vitamin C, 1000 mg four times a day. Increase your water intake in order to loosen the phlegm and make your cough more effective. Other herbal-type remedies, such as garlic, can be added at your discretion. To address your symptoms, take medications to relieve the pain and fever. Aspirin and ibuprofen are better than acetaminophen, provided there are no contraindications (such as a history of bleeding or stomach ulcers).

Relieve the sore throat by gargling with warm salt water or drinking hot ginger tea. You can even keep a mug of this beside you on stage – audiences are used to performers sipping between songs.

You should take a cough suppressant only when needed, keeping in mind that these are often a bit drying, and also that apart from when you're singing or sleeping, that cough may not be bad thing: it clears your chest of infection.

Next, adjust your set to reflect the temporary impairment of your condition. If you have the option of shortening the set, taking out songs that are especially demanding, tweaking the sound system, or adding more instrumental bits, do it - anything to reduce the amount of high-strain singing is recommended.

Finally, once your gig is over, take a break! Your immune system is working hard to get you better, and you should not sabotage that effort by pretending that everything is fine.

Rhinitis is Ruining my Range!

Dear Doctor Jahn,

I have lost my top for the past two weeks - no throat pain, but if I try to sing in my upper range, I cannot get a single sound out (except for wheezy air). This has happened to me several times before, but it usually lasts a week. After the week passed, I went to a doctor on Wednesday. He diagnosed me with chronic rhinitis (chronic postnasal drip). He prescribed me a steroid nasal spray. He also told me it would probably take another two weeks before I can get my voice back. Do many other singers suffer from this? Can you give me a few pointers on how to take care of my voice right now, as well as some suggestions on how to try to avoid the rhinitis happening again? - Rosalind

Dear Rosalind,

Rhinitis and postnasal drip are common, and normally do not cause the symptoms you have described. Did the doctor look at your vocal folds? It sounds to me like you have some swelling that prevents the folds from approximating and thinning out (i.e. loss of flexibility) at the high range. Other possibilities, such as a hemorrhage, can only be ruled out by laryngoscopy. It is also possible that you have strained the muscles (muscle tension dysphonia), although with this condition the mix is more affected than the top.

Preventing postnasal drip is a topic unto itself. Drinking a lot of water, identifying and avoiding (or treating) inhalant allergens, and twice daily saline washes using a Neti pot or a squeeze bottle like NeilMed would be a good place to start.

Can Constant Illness Damage My Voice Forever?

Dear Dr. Jahn,

I've been sick for a long time – first with a sore throat followed by an infection. Then, I suffered with allergies and now I'm sick again! I tried singing earlier today and it sounded really bad – do you think I have messed up my voice? How would I know if I have done any permanent damage? - Rosa

Dear Rosa,

You seem to be asking two questions. First, why are you sick all the time? And then, does singing while you are sick damage your voice? Your two "illnesses", the sore throat and then the allergies, may be connected or separate from each other. Sore throats can result from an infection, either viral or bacterial. These occur after exposure to an infectious agent (bacterium or virus), but if they occur frequently, you need to look to your immune system.

Are you getting enough good food, rest and exercise? Are you under chronic physical and psychological stress? All of these predispose you to getting frequent infections. For most bugs, it takes two to tango: the bug and your weakened immune system. While you may not be able to predict or limit your exposure to infection, taking care of your general health and maintaining a strong immune system is entirely within your control! Allergies are not a sign of a weak immune system, rather of an immune system that is overreacting to the wrong things.

This is something that you can address by finding out what you might be allergic to, avoiding exposure (if it is cats, then keep your cat out of the bedroom), and taking appropriate medications to minimize your allergy symptoms. And here is where the two conditions come together: allergic symptoms can stress your body and make you more vulnerable to infections. Your body may be dealing with two crises at the same time, an inflammatory response to the allergen as well as to the infectious agent. Also consider that if allergies block your nose, you may breathe through your mouth more, inviting bugs to take up residence in your pharynx.

Now, your voice: When you are sick, either with allergy or infection, it will impair your singing and change how you use your vocal apparatus to produce your voice. This compensatory behavior usually stops once your vocal tract is healthy again. It may, however, persist as a new bad habit, and now the compensation becomes the disease. So, after you are healthy again and your voice is not, visit your teacher and do a thorough check up on your voice, resetting your singing technique to its pre-illness norm.

If your voice does not recover between episodes of sickness, you will need to see an ear, nose and throat doctor who specializes in the voice to make sure that there has been no structural damage to your larynx.

How Soon Will My Voice Return After Illness?

Dear Doctor Jahn,

After I've had a cold or cough, once the congestion and coughing are completely gone, how much longer should it take for my voice to go back to normal, provided that I'm not singing? What If I AM singing? - George

Dear George,

In general, once your symptoms are fully gone, you should be back to normal singing within 5-7 days. However, this is not always so, and you need to consider several aspects of your sickness and your vocal behavior. If your infection was accompanied by a great deal of coughing or throat pain, this may have resulted in some residual swelling of the vocal folds, which will become apparent if you try to sing softly in your falsetto.

Coughing also causes the larynx to rise in the neck, and in this higher laryngeal position it may be difficult to smoothly negotiate the mix.

The main problem really is trying to get back to normal too early. By forcing the mechanism to produce a sound that you recognize as normal, you may be engaging excessive muscle effort.

This increases tension in the larynx and the pharynx, and can lead to a new and forced type of phonation that is harmful and in fact unnecessary once the cold is gone.

Approach your cold with three ideas. First, do whatever you can to hasten its progress and resolution, while minimizing voice use. Let your body deal with the infection with, of course, your additional measures of Vitamin C, zinc, and other remedies that you have found helpful.
Second, if you do need to perform with a cold, drastically alter your expectations of yourself, and be conscious of which additional mechanisms you have temporarily engaged to get through the performance.

Finally, once the cold is over, revert to your normal good technique - if it doesn't return spontaneously, vocalize a bit more and go back to your teacher for a one lesson check-up and brush-up. If, with all of this, your voice continues to be hoarse, consider a medical examination of your larynx.

What's the Safest Way to Clear My Throat?

Dr. Jahn,

So what's the deal about clearing an itchy throat? I've heard that its "bad" to clear your throat with an "Ahem!" Is that really true? - Allan

Dear Allan,

Occasional throat clearing, used to dislodge mucus from the throat or vocal folds, is not harmful. When throat clearing becomes habitual, however, there is a concern that forcefully grinding the vocal folds together may cause some damage. This damage is usually not on the soft membranous part of the vocal folds (the part that vibrates with singing), but toward the back, where the folds consist of a thin membrane covering firm cartilage. Excessive rubbing here can damage the mucous membrane and expose the cartilage, causing irritation, pain and inflammatory tissue formation.

I would suggest that you try to find out why you need to habitually clear your throat – allergies, reflux, or a nervous habit? Consider food sensitivities - especially a dairy allergy - or excessive sweets. Any of these may cause mucus to thicken and adhere to your vocal folds. Then, by addressing the various possible causes, you may be able to get rid of potentially harmful chronic clearing.

Seeking a Magical Cure for My Throat Infection

Dear Doctor Jahn,

I haven't been sick for years! I don't have time to be: I gig 6 nights a week! But here I am with a temperature (102), sore throat, stuck in bed for the second day. I want an instant cure! Short of that, tell me the quickest way I can get through this and back up on stage!! - Janine

Dear Janine,

No matter what great health you enjoy, you will inevitably occasionally get sick. So if you gig six nights a week and haven't been sick for years, isn't it time that you were? I mean, you need to cut yourself a bit of slack. Fever is not the illness, but it is your immune system's response to a bacterial or viral invader. So if you get a fever, especially a brief episode, it is just a sign that your immune system is doing a good job - it is raising your body temperature to make the environment too hot for those bugs.

My suggestion is to not ignore or suppress your symptoms just to get back on stage, but rather that you support your body in the war effort by resting, drinking lots of water and taking Vitamin C - at least 1000 mg a day, which you can increase to 4000 mg a day while you're sick.

Your illness sounds like an acute bacterial infection, so you may also consider antibiotics if you're not getting better on your own within 3-4 days.

More importantly, once this episode is gone, consider on-going preventive methods, including regular exercise, vitamins, a healthy diet and adequate rest. Can you get on stage and perform with a raging fever? You could, by dosing up on aspirin and other drugs. But unless you're doing it to get through an uncancellable career-defining performance opportunity, why would you? You're short-changing your body and undermining your general health by doing so.

Have Throat Germs Travelled Down to my Voice?

Dear Doctor Jahn,

I was diagnosed with strep throat about two weeks ago. The sore throat was gone after about five days on antibiotics, and after one week, I started singing again. I was hoarse from the start. I stopped and tried again one week later. Again, I was hoarse after about 15 minutes.

I've always had a very healthy voice. Can strep affect the vocal cords? I'm worried I might have done damage.
- Petra

Dear Petra,

Normally strep should not affect the vocal cords. If you had a strep infection of the larynx, you would have much more severe symptoms, so this is not due to the strep. It is however possible that if you were singing with an infected throat, you were straining to phonate and this muscled type of phonation has persisted now that the infection is gone. I would have your larynx examined and then work on singing without tension and with as much support as you can.

How to Treat Freshman's Flu

Dear Doctor Jahn,

My daughter is studying voice and is a freshman this year. She just got sick and it looks like she has a common cold (sneezing, coughing, and her throat hurts). She went to Health Services on campus. She doesn't have strep (she had a test done) and the doctor thinks it is a cold. The doctor suggested she take Sudafed and told her she should not take Nyquil or Dayquil as it will affect her vocal cords. Also, he told her that she should not take Echinacea or Airborne, as she is already sick and it will only poison her body. Is he correct? What over-the-counter medication could you recommend in the situation of the common cold? I appreciate your advice very much. - Lisa

Dear Lisa,

I wonder about the medical advice your daughter received. I happen to like Airborne—it is a combination of vitamins and antioxidants that, from personal experience, can shorten a cold. I am particularly puzzled by the doctor's choice of words: "poisoned" seems rather harsh when you're talking about Vitamin C!

Here are some of the measures your daughter can take. To avoid a cold, she should take vitamins daily, especially during cold season. This includes a multivitamin and vitamin C, 1,000 mg. a day. She needs to get enough rest, eat well, and in general maintain her immune system. When she feels a cold starting, I suggest increasing vitamin C to 4,000 mg. a day in divided doses, as well as using Zicam nasal swabs. Zinc, as nasal swabs or tablets, has been shown to reduce the duration, severity, and infectivity of rhinoviruses. She of course needs to stay warm and drink plenty of fluids when a cold starts. Rest also is important—you should not exercise in an attempt to drive the cold out.

The only possible problem with Dayquil or Nyquil is that they contain antihistamines, which are drying to the vocal cords—a temporary and harmless side effect.

Consider also that the strep test does not rule out any of several other bacteria that can cause a throat infection. If she is coughing or blowing out colored mucus, I would consider treatment with antibiotics, regardless of the strep test.

How Can I Cure my Lengthy Laryngitis?

Dear Doctor Jahn,

I've had a bad cold, then laryngitis, but I still have it after five weeks! I sound terrible. I've been doing the normal vocal rest, plenty of fluids, etc. I think I'm getting a little better. I'm on Biaxin. Have you ever heard of laryngitis going on this long? - Brian

Dear Brian,

Persistent hoarseness after a cold could be due to several factors. If all of the cold symptoms have resolved except for the hoarseness, the most likely cause is abnormal posturing of the larynx. During the cold, if the singer continues to try to sing, he or she may need to "muscle" the voice more to try to get an acceptable sound. This excess muscle tension usually involves squeezing or grabbing at the laryngeal level. After several days, this adaptation becomes "the norm," and the singer unconsciously uses excessive laryngeal pressure. As the cold resolves, adaptation becomes maladaptation. It must therefore be consciously un-learned, concentrating on releasing tension in the neck, lowering the larynx and opening the back of the throat. A good voice therapist can be helpful with this. We also see this situation after colds which involve a lot of coughing.

Less common causes of persistent hoarseness are hemorrhage of the vocal fold from coughing and gastroesophageal reflux (GERD), particularly when the illness involves gastrointestinal symptoms such as regurgitation and vomiting.

How Can I Deal with Marathon Colds?

Dear Doctor Jahn,

I have had a cold for nearly a week: four days of sore throat, three days (and possibly more) of streaming nose, to be followed by up to two or three weeks of heavy chest congestion. Most of my colds last six weeks.

I have a gig in a month and there is no cover, no substitute singer. How does one cope with a cold once it starts to run its normal course, which can take several weeks? - Anne-Marie

Dear Anne-Marie,

In my experience, colds should not last several weeks; if they do, I wonder about your general state of immunity and health. If you do have a cold that seems to linger, try Zinc gluconate (oral tablets or nasal swabs). This can shorten a cold, make it less severe and make you less contagious. High doses of vitamin C (4 to 8 grams in divided doses) also help. Don't exercise or try to "work through" your cold—let your body deal with it. Drink lots of water. Assuming your immune system works normally, you should be fine within a couple of weeks. Don't sing too much with your cold, since you may get into bad posturing habits that you will have to learn to undo later.

3. Perfect Vocal Care

Do I Really Need to Take Care of My Voice?

Dear Doctor Jahn,

To be honest, I'm grossed out by the thought of nasal sprays and sitting around with a steamer doesn't fit my sense of how I want to spend my evening. Are these things really necessary to get the most out of my voice?
- Gary

Dear Gary,

I appreciate the sense of your comments; it is not my intention to suggest that good singing necessarily requires elaborate rituals of daily hygiene. And the truth is that many singers - especially in the non-classical genres - just sing, taking their voice for granted as a God-given talent.

So if you are a singer who sings consistently well by dint of natural ability and hard work, the last thing you want to do is to fuss and obsess with your voice! But if your voice is your livelihood, you need it to be good and dependable – not now and then, but every time.

There are only a few professions where your reputation and your pay check are on the line each and every time you do your work – singing is one of them. Think of your vocal apparatus as your car, a machine that you drive hard, day after day. You can maintain it, or you can fix it. The one thing you cannot do, in this case, is trade it in! You're stuck with this one car for the rest of your life.

If you want it to dependably take you where you need to go, ongoing maintenance is the obvious answer! It is inexpensive and harmless to maintain your voice - although, I agree, a bit boring. Steaming, drinking lots of water and periods of voice rest are not sexy. But trying to fix the voice once it's broken is not only more expensive but also unpredictable. Either way, it's the one voice you have.

As a famous opera singer once said, you should always sing on the interest, not on the principal. Don't "spend" your vocal capital, because once it is gone, once you have run out of ways to compensate for a voice that is irretrievably damaged, you may be stuck.

What is Vocal Rest and When Should I Do It?

Dear Doctor Jahn,

I've heard so many singers and coaches speak about "vocal rest" But how do I "rest" my voice? No singing? No talking? No loud singing? Those all sound impossible options for me, given my schedule and obligations!
- Kerry

Dear Kerry,

There are many types of vocal rest. Absolute rest of course refers to not uttering a word.
Patients who have hemorrhaged into the vocal folds are advised to do this.

I tell such patients that the only thing they're allowed to say is "The house is on fire!" – otherwise, complete silence.

A voiced whisper, by the way, is not a substitute for vocal rest. Of course, absolute voice rest is punishingly difficult, and usually not necessary.

If you have a swelling of the vocal folds, modified vocal rest is the answer. Do not sing, and minimize speaking to situations where it is absolutely necessary. Avoid social interactions, particularly in a noisy environment. If necessary, speak one-on-one to someone, using a "confidential" voice. This is an easier prescription, particularly in the age of computers and text messaging.

An even less difficult form of voice rest is to avoid singing with vocal strain. For vocal performers this ideally means speaking in head voice and avoiding belting, loud and high singing, and doing longer performances or multiple sets. This is appropriate for singers with vocal nodules.

There are a few more things to understand about vocal rest. When you rest your voice for more than two days, the larynx begins to rise in the neck. For classical singers this is an issue, since they are trained to keep the larynx low. But even for non-classical singers, expect whatever laryngeal posturing you may have learned to revert to its pre-training, "natural" position.

So, coming off voice rest, give yourself some time to reposition your larynx in its "normal" singing posture. Also, if you are using voice rest to reverse damage from chronic voice abuse such as nodules, rest is not enough – you need to work on the technical problems that caused the damage in the first place.

Nodules may decrease or even disappear with voice rest, but will return quickly if you do not modify the vocal behavior that caused them in the first place.

Voice rest, then, can be absolute or relative. While small periods of rest can work wonders, it is not a cure-all, and generally should not be recommended for more than a week at most.

How Can I Get a Voice Doctor Appointment?

Dear Doctor Jahn,

How do I convince my G.P. to refer me to an Ear, Nose & Throat specialist to look at my vocal cords? My appointment with my E.N.T. is 2 months away! Where can I get help for my vocal problems between now and then?
- Kerry

Dear Kerry,

I am assuming that you are in the U.K., dealing with the bureaucracy and overutilization inherent in the National Health System. In the USA, you could be seen within a week, particularly in high-doctor-density locations like New York.

You didn't tell us whether you are having vocal problems, or are just curious to get a baseline examination of your larynx. If you are well, with no symptoms such as hoarseness, difficulty swallowing, coughing or spitting up blood, then a two-month wait is probably acceptable.

If, on the other hand, you are experiencing hoarseness - particularly hoarseness that is not getting better or is worsening - along with other symptoms that would suggest a problem in the throat, then you should be seen sooner.

I would assume you could see a consultant using private insurance, or by paying for your visit, although I am not that familiar with the U.K. health system.

In general, however, if your voice is fine or has not changed recently, and you don't have any other signs or symptoms suggestive of a progressively worsening condition, you may need to just wait.

Saline Nasal Flushing Feels like Drowning!

Dear Doctor Jahn,

Inspired by the brief article about Neti pots, I trekked to my local health food store to buy a Neti pot, brought it home, and followed the detailed instructions. Knocked over by a big wave while swimming as a child, I first felt the sensation of salt water in my nasal passages. With the Neti pot, I rediscovered that sensation. It's hard to imagine a more unpleasant daily cleansing ritual. Forcing salt water through my nose feels absolutely awful in every way. After the sordid ordeal is over, and the dust and impurities have been gently washed away, my mucous membranes protest at having been so impolitely violated, and react by producing more mucus. I actually end up more congested than before I began. It's been over a month now, and I'm giving up. Some ancient yogi is having a good belly laugh at his practical joke. - Dina

Dear Dina,

I'm sorry you have had problems with the Neti pot. I have recommended it to my patients for years, and most of them find it very useful. A couple of suggestions for your next nasal adventure: try to adjust the concentration of salt so it is neither too strong nor too weak. If in doubt, try buying physiologic or normal saline at the drug store. This has the same concentration of salt as your body fluids, and should not be irritating. Second, when you pour the solution into your nostril, tip your head both to the side and slightly forward. This will ensure that the solution goes into (and out through) the other nostril, and not into your throat or ears. Also, pour slowly! You control the flow with your hand. Your experience, while not unheard of, is not typical. Give it another try. If it doesn't work for you, you may want to consult an otolaryngologist to see whether you might have a septal deviation, which misdirects the flow of the solution. If none of this helps, consider switching to a large squeeze bottle like NeilMed, which you can do upright over a sink.

Meditation Chanting: Good or Bad for my Voice?

Dear Doctor Jahn,

I have just begun a meditation practice that involves chanting 20 minutes on "ah" in the morning, and 20 minutes on "om" in the evening. (Paraphrasing Irving Berlin, "I got the 'ah' in the morning and the 'om' at night.") Each 20-minute period is to be divided into one-third medium loud, one-third medium soft, and one-third silent. I wonder if chanting one pitch only for a sustained period, and first thing in the morning upon rising, will be hard on my voice? - Jasmine

Dear Jasmine,

I love your Berlin paraphrase. From the medical point of view, I really don't think chanting should hurt your voice, providing it is at a comfortable pitch and not an excessive volume. The pitch should probably be in chest voice, at least a third below the register change, and well supported (i.e. floating on the breath and not pushed). In terms of dynamics, chanting turns your mind inward, and you will quickly become focused on the breath and the sensation of vibration in the chest, so I suspect you will not push or hurt yourself.

You might be interested to read about the five tones in Chinese medicine, each corresponding to a specific organ. The Chinese say you can strengthen solid (zhang) organs in the body by chanting different tones. The truth is, you can find out only by doing it. You will certainly not physically hurt yourself by trying. If you find there is any adverse effect on your voice, you could consider other forms of meditation, such as qigong.

Happy humming, and consider adding "Some en-chanted evening" to your repertoire...

Vocal Weakness After Illness – What's Going On?

Dear Doctor Jahn,

I am a teacher and singer – as a result I don't have much chance to rest my voice. 2 months ago I had a cold, lost my voice and since then have found that both my speaking and singing voice have not recovered their full strength. Talking for too long is uncomfortable. I have seen a local GP and he advises nothing is wrong and that I should rest. It's impossible for me to not speak for more than a few days at the moment. How do I get my voice back? - Jean

Dear Jean,

There could be several reasons for your situation. I am assuming your cold and its symptoms have completely resolved and you are back to full health again. One possibility is that during your cold, between coughing and either vocal rest or abnormally strained voice use, you have changed how you phonate.

If your larynx is high and you are phonating with excessive laryngeal tension (muscling the voice rather than supporting it from below), you may experience discomfort after singing, as well as a weaker and more strained voice. This latter symptom often occurs when the larynx is elevated and the resonating compartments above the larynx are overly constricted. If you have any residual pulmonary issues, you may not be breathing freely or supporting the voice adequately.

If you are generally more fatigued, I would suggest a test for infection mono (Epstein-Barr virus), which can leave you with general weakness for months.

Finally, it is possible that the virus has weakened one of the nerves going to the larynx.

This would make it difficult to close the vocal folds and lead to excessive (and sub-optimally efficient) efforts at vocalizing.

One particular form of nerve weakness (superior laryngeal nerve palsy) affects the head voice preferentially, and will leave you with an intact chest voice but problems above the mix.

My suggestion after reviewing the above list is that you consult an otolaryngologist (an ear, nose and throat doctor) for a specialist's expert opinion.

The Side Effects of Cigarettes

Dear Doctor Jahn,

I am a professional singer but I am also a smoker (10 cigarettes per day for 8 years.) My current age is 30. Would you please give me your thoughts on how smoking can affect my voice, and most of all what are the benefits I will draw if I quit? I really need your opinion. Are there other singers who smoke? And can you give any examples? Many thanks. - Paul

Dear Paul,

It is true that many singers in the past have been smokers. Enrico Caruso, Frank Sinatra and Adele smoked for a time. But these performers have sung well despite this deleterious habit. You should be singing at your best, rather than succeeding in spite of a self-imposed handicap.

In brief, smoking involves inhaling tar, nicotine and other toxic matter into your lungs. Over the long term, lung tissue is damaged, and this impairs your breath control, even during normal breathing (chronic obstructive lung disease).

The bronchi and trachea can clear some debris by means of tiny cilia that sweep things up and out of the lungs. But nicotine paralyses the cilia, so the tar stays around. You can only get rid of the stuff by coughing it up, another potentially damaging manoeuvre. Additionally, smoke is drying and carcinogenic. Even if you escape the big 'C', you might develop chronic edema of the vocal folds (called Reinke's edema), resulting in lowered pitch, loss of high notes and generalized raspiness which may not completely resolve even if you stop smoking.

It is historically interesting that in the past, when people were observed coughing up sputum after smoking, the connection was not made. In fact, there was even a suggestion that smoking is good for your lungs because it triggers a cough which gets rid of sputum! Of course, this misconception was perpetuated by tobacco companies. Somehow, they never made the connection that it was the smoking that produced the sputum.

Again, many singers smoke, but you will in the long run do better if you quit. You will have a longer career, with a better voice in your later years. I would also say that if you smoke only 10 cigarettes a day, it shouldn't be hard to quit, at least from the physical/addiction aspect.

How Do I Un-Wax my Ears?

Dear Doctor Jahn,

About six months ago after cleaning out my ears with Q-tips, my right ear plugged up that night while I was sleeping. The next morning when I got up, it unplugged after about 5 minutes being upright. It has continued to do this off and on ever since. It always unplugs in the morning after a few minutes, so I haven't really worried about it. What do you think caused this, and what can I do to resolve it? Should I use some sort of at-home earwax removal system, and do they really work? Or do I need to see a doctor? - Alex

Dear Alex,

The ear canals of most people constantly produce wax, a greasy secretion that forms in the outer part of the canal and eventually hardens and drops out. If you clean your ears with Q-tips, there is a possibility of pushing the wax in, toward the eardrum. If you occlude the canal completely, you will feel a blockage. However, if you occlude the canal only, say, 90 percent, your hearing will be normal until that last 10 percent is blocked—from the hearing point of view, a partial occlusion has no effect: it's either blocked or not. When you sleep, and especially if you sleep with your ears buried in the pillow, the wax may melt a bit and move around. This can complete the blockage and cause a hearing loss.

Two other possible causes should be considered. Lying flat can cause some redistribution of fluids in the body and a slight swelling in the canal (consider how swelling around the ankles disappears overnight). Finally, using Q-tips can cause a low-level irritation in the ear canals with edema, again narrowing the canal.

And that's probably way more than you needed to know! But if the blockage persists or recurs, I would see an ENT doctor. They have access to a microscope (family practitioners don't) and can more thoroughly inspect the deep ear canal.

There are Gigs in the Diary and My Voice is Raspy!

Dear Doctor Jahn,

For some strange reason I've lost my upper range and my lower range is quite raspy–I am currently scheduled to sing a pop concert, using my upper range, with a local symphony in two months! Their press goes out in a week. Do I hope for improvement and everything works out? Do I let the symphony know in advance of predicament? I don't have a cold or flu. My voice, throat, vocal cords, etc. do not hurt. - Candice

Dear Candice,

For a well-trained singer performing legitimate repertoire, this might be a loss of the higher notes from swelling, which in turn could be from excessive singing, overexertion or other factors that can alter the surface of the vocal folds.

Allergies are a common co-factor which can thicken your mucus and cause mild swelling of the vocal tract, making it more difficult and effortful to produce a voice. If you keep singing and trying to push through, the compensatory manoeuvre is to overly squeeze the vocal folds together and "muscle" the voice.

This, in turn, will start to affect the lower range of the voice and cause hoarseness, starting in the mix and eventually involving the lower voice as well.

It is also possible that you have a severe enough inflammation of the larynx that the inflammation itself has caused hoarseness throughout the range.

Once infection and reflux have been ruled out, and depending on your physical examination, I might suggest a course of cortisone by mouth, and the use of an inhaler that includes saline, cortisone, and a vasoconstrictor such as Neo-Synephrine.

I would certainly advise the sponsors that you are having vocal difficulties; even if you can perform, they should have a back-up plan. This is a case where an examination is really the way forward. I would suggest that you get to your local laryngologist right away for a definitive diagnosis.

Need a Speedy Recovery After Demanding Gig!

Dear Doctor Jahn,

If I occasionally beat up my voice, how much rest does it need to recover? Two days of gentle voice use? More? I am talking about the other night when I strained my voice at a three-hour gig with a bad sound system and ended up with a raspy voice at the end of it. - Samuel

Dear Samuel,

I wish there were a simple formula I could give you. In reality, there are too many factors at play. Your age, the anatomical attributes of your vocal equipment, your general health, state of hydration, non-singing vocal habits, social factors (smoking and drinking), as well as what actually happened to your cords – just some factors to consider. Huskiness from a bit of swelling or muscle strain is quite different from hoarseness due to a vocal cord hemorrhage.

Here are some suggestions. If you have significantly strained your voice, try 48 hours of complete voice rest. This means no singing, no talking, and only essential minimal whispering (not the stressful "stage whisper"). Stay well hydrated during this time. Then, try vocalizing. Try some soft sirens (glissandos) up and down to check the top and the mix. Be aware of, and avoid, compensating by muscling or squeezing the voice if the top is clear but the mix is problematic; try muscle relaxing techniques such as stretching and massaging the neck.

The best, of course, is to avoid the situation. Like most things, if vocal strain becomes the norm rather than the exception, consider seeing a vocal coach to ensure that your singing technique is not the source of your vocal strain.

How Can I Sober Up My Voice?

Dear Doctor Jahn,

I had two shots of alcohol when I went out with some friends last night, and I have to sing Thursday. The alcohol isn't out of my system yet and my voice sounds

terrible. How can I get the alcohol out of my system by Thursday? Is it possible? - Jessica

Dear Jessica,

Today being Wednesday, I would assume that the alcohol will be gone by Thursday, if it was only one or two shots. With such a relatively small amount of alcohol, most of the effects are due to dehydration: alcohol acts as a diuretic (it increases urine output) and can leave you and your vocal apparatus dry. Drink lots of water to rehydrate, and try to get some moderate exercise today (not exhaustive- like vigorous walking for about an hour). Going forward, please rehydrate when drinking alcohol, and you should be able to avoid "vocal hangover".

Why Is There So Much "Air" In My Tone?

Dear Doctor Jahn,

I was wondering what could be wrong with my vocal cords and what I should do. I am a music major and lately when I sing in the upper register, I can hit the notes but as the note sounds, I can also hear air coming through. It's like the note and a hissing of air. Should I just go on vocal rest and drink plenty of water and will this subside? - Anne

Dear Anne,

Your description certainly suggests that the vocal folds are not meeting in the middle, particularly in the top register. I would be interested to know how your voice behaves at the register shift (passaggio). This is usually the area where muscle tension manifests.

If the problem is only at the top, swellings or possibly nodules may indeed be the cause. If, on the other hand, the voice is breathy throughout its range and especially if you're having problems at the register shift, the muscle tension may also play a role.

Regarding management, there should be no problem with voice rest for a week. If the voice improves and returns to normal, then nothing more needs to be done. If the breathiness persists, however, then you should see a doctor and have the larynx examined.

4. Keep Your Energy Up!

Can I Energize My Old Tired Voice?

Dear Doctor Jahn,

I am likely what you call an "under-trained" beginning singer, having started my career as a cantorial soloist five years ago, at age 55. As a result of overuse—and too much travel and performance three months ago in dry climates over a short period of time, coupled with a minor chest infection and major laryngitis—I was left with "burn out," a failing speaking voice, and diagnosed with reflux and fatigue. My voice now tires after even just talking for over an hour, and I feel a general low grade irritation in my throat, along with neck tension. My ENT examination was normal: nothing to see in the larynx. Apart from rest and gentle vocalizing, is there anything else I can do? - Vivian

Dear Vivian,

First, I commend you on your decision to pursue a career that you obviously enjoy, even at the age of 55. Many singers never do this, and spend their lives regretting it. Based on what you've told me, I think you need to consider several possibilities:

1. Overuse, compounded by excess muscle tension. This, in turn, may be due to inadequate training in basic vocal technique. Lessons and practice should help.

2. Menopause and general mucosal dryness, which can compound muscle tension (trying to overcome vocal difficulties).

3. General health issues need to be checked, such as mild hypothyroidism, anemia, or chronic inflammation. These are all conditions that are easy to diagnose with blood tests, and can be

treated. You may also benefit from acupuncture and Chinese herbs, and should consider this if your blood tests do not point to a specific medical problem.

Good luck, and let me know how you fare!

Brandy OK as Part of my Pre-Gig Warm up?

Dear Doctor Jahn,

When I get sick, I typically drink a shot of Grand Marnier to warm things up. Seems to work ok, but I'm wondering if I'm doing damage from this practice? Is there a better quick remedy for getting through a rough night? - Robert

Dear Robert,

Certainly a small amount of alcohol should not be harmful, everything else being normal.

Gargling with port has been passed down anecdotally as a good warm-up used by old-time British actors. My guess is that the gargle was usually followed by a swallow...

Alcohol has numerous effects which may be helpful in your situation. First, it is a peripheral vasodilator; this means it increases the circulation to your mucous membranes, as well as your skin (manifesting as facial flushing). Taken in excess, it could potentially cause some swelling of the throat but, again, a small amount should be fine. If "getting sick" in your case refers to an upper respiratory tract infection, remember that you already have some swelling in the vocal tract, and further relaxing the blood vessels in this area could increase that swelling.

Second, alcohol is slightly disinhibiting, and can help to calm any performance anxiety. Once more, larger amounts can impair your artistic judgment, but quantity is the key here. A couple of words of caution: alcohol in larger quantities is a diuretic, and can leave your vocal folds dry and more vulnerable. It can also act as an anaesthetic and blunt the throat's warning signs when you potentially over-sing.

But you do have good taste! You could be gargling with Bulmer's Woodpecker cider!

How Sick Does a Singer Have to be to Stop Singing?

Dear Doctor Jahn,

One of my very enthusiastic college freshman students has been diagnosed with mononucleosis. I know that the symptoms include sore throat, fatigue, fever, and swollen, tender lymph nodes. I also know that it is contagious and that it takes about six weeks to be completely over it.

As her teacher, I am wondering whether it's OK for her to proceed with lessons if her throat doesn't hurt at the time, or if it would be better for her to just drop lessons this semester (which would be very upsetting to her). Also, as a professional singer with engagements coming up soon, I am always concerned about my own health. Should I be concerned about teaching her (assuming I am not up in her face or touching her, but merely spending time in the same small studio)? - Kate

Dear Kate,

Infectious mono is contagious and is spread through physical contact and saliva. First, for yourself, I would just get a blood test for Epstein-Barr virus titers. Most likely you have had it already and should be immune. If the titer is negative for you (meaning never infected), I would be careful. For your student; if she feels OK she can continue lessons, but don't push—some cases go on to Chronic Fatigue Syndrome. Of course, early on after infection, she may just be too ill to sing. Also, early in the infection, it is not uncommon for the tonsils to be massively enlarged, which would also interfere with singing.

Can a Vegetarian Rock the Stage?

Dear Doctor Jahn,

Many of my friends in the arts scene are vegetarians; I'm attracted to the idea. But the thing is, I'm a hard rocker, use tons of physical energy on stage and I don't want to compromise my health in any way. Is it possible to have a perfectly healthy diet and be a vegetarian or am I heading down an endless road of supplements and dangers? There's just so much propaganda on this issue and I was hoping you could clear the air. - Alan

Dear Alan,

This is a great question and one for which there is no real answer, short of personal experience.

But I would re-phrase it: can a vegetarian get enough nutrition from a diet that lacks meat? It seems to me that as long as you get the right amount (and the correct ratio) of carbohydrates, protein and fats, it shouldn't make a difference whether they derive from animal or vegetarian sources. Of the three, fats have the highest number of calories per weight (of food consumed) so this would have to figure into your diet. Surprisingly, though, fats do occur in vegetarian food such as nuts.

Protein is found in many non-meat sources, most notably in soy, while the best quick source of energy is simple carbohydrates - the sugars found in fruit, for example - so you should be okay in that regard. You would, however, be likely to need to eat a greater volume of food to get all of the nutrition you need. As you're unlikely to sing well on a full stomach, I would recommend eating smaller amounts more frequently. This "grazing" style of eating is actually healthier than the usual three meals a day.

Now the really interesting question is: will you sing with as much passion and aggressive energy if you don't eat meat? Soy, the main source of protein in most vegetarian diets, is a prime source of the female hormone estrogen (called phytoestrogen) and for this reason it is often recommended to post-menopausal women. Would substituting estrogen-laden tofu for red meat change the masculine energy of your performance?

As I said, there is no real answer short of trying this, but do let me (and other readers) know!

Should I be a Vocal Athlete?

Dear Doctor Jahn,

I'm getting more into singing (my band is starting to get several gigs a week) and I am thinking I should "up" my fitness a bit. The thing is, I have a group of friends who are "fitness freaks" and each into something different – one swears by Pilates, another weightlifting, another running etc.! I figure it doesn't really matter what it is – but you work with singers all the time – what is your recommendation?! - Eric

Dear Eric,

Your question is deceptively simple, and is asking for a long reply, but I will try to answer it in kind. Really, any physical exercise that you enjoy and can commit to doing regularly should serve your purposes.

They key is the commitment, mentally and schedule-wise. It cannot be something you do "in your spare time", but needs to be high priority. This way you will experience the cumulative benefits to your body, your singing, and your psychological health. More specifically, your exercise should address three areas: cardiovascular health, muscle toning, and flexibility. You can attain all three by one exercise such as swimming, or by a combination of methods such as jogging, weights and stretching. How you succeed, however, will again depend on your sticking to it. This is why your regimen should consist of things you like to do – you won't persist if it's a chore!

Regular exercise (ideally five times a week for an hour) that raises your heart rate into your optimal zone, which is *(220 – your age) x 80%*, should be your goal, followed by toning (weights, machines, sit-ups, curls, etc.) and stretching. You'll feel better, metabolize more effectively, and be a happier singer!

Exhaustion Affecting Singing Stamina

Dear Doctor Jahn,

Yesterday one of my returning voice students had her first lesson of the new academic year. She became lightheaded and things began to go black as we were vocalizing. She sat down immediately and as the minutes passed, she said her ears felt as if they needed to pop—as if she had been flying. Last spring in her lessons she became light headed once or twice, but it was weeks into the term when she was run

down and lacking sleep, so I was not overly concerned. Since yesterday was only the second day of classes, there wasn't time to be exhausted yet, and the need for her ears to pop was a new experience. Could you share with us your thoughts on this situation? - Linda

Dear Linda,

This is an interesting problem which may have several causes. Let me ask you a couple of questions first. Does your student have low blood pressure? Has she lost a lot of weight over the summer or is she dieting aggressively? The clinical picture you are so clearly describing suggests primarily that your student is hyperventilating when she is singing. If she does not breathe well through her nose and is gasping for air or going through the breath too quickly, she may be hyperventilating—blowing off too much carbon dioxide when she is singing. A simple test for this would be to ask her to breathe quickly and deeply through the mouth 20 times, and see whether this reproduces her symptoms. If she tells you that her lips and fingertips tingle as she is about to black out during singing, this would also support the hyperventilation theory.

Low blood pressure may also cause a sensation of fainting, especially when she stands for longer periods of time. General weakness from excessive dieting and weight loss is another possibility. Sudden excessive weight loss impairs abdominal support and can change breathing patterns. Finally, with excessive rapid weight loss, the Eustachian tubes of the ears can become floppy (they also lose support!), and a sensation of ear blockage can develop.

What to do? Ask her to see her doctor to check blood pressure while sitting and standing to determine if there is significant postural drop. Ask her to do a blood count to see whether she is anemic. If everything mentioned above checks out, she should do some vocal exercises where she sings slow, soft, and sustained passages to train a gradual release of the breath without pushing too much air. This may help.

Can I Swim Then Sing?

Dear Doctor Jahn,

I recently have been snorkelling in a pool at a local recreation center. I love swimming. It is the only exercise that I can do. However, I am getting very dry during the workout and my voice seems challenged lately. The swimming is a new variable in my life, so it seems plausible that there is a cause and effect. However, I thought I would get your opinion. - Jamie

Dear Jamie,

I am not an expert on diving or snorkelling, but my first thought would be that breathing through your mouth for any reason (including using the snorkel equipment) would cause the vocal tract to dry out. Normally, we are not meant to breathe through our mouth, but through our nose. The nose is designed to take in air and in a matter of a couple of inches, warm it to body temperature and fully humidify it — the mouth cannot do this.

Something similar occurs in patients who mouth breathe or snore at night—they wake up with a throat that is dry and even sore. This occurs even during sleep, when we are at rest and not exerting ourselves. Add to this the increase in airflow as you exert yourself under water (and the additional effort imposed by having to clear the "dead space" of the snorkel tube with each breath), and you have a problem. A further consideration is the fact that the air just above the pool surface may contain some chlorinated water aerosol, which is an irritant to your mucous membranes.

The most logical solution is to drink lots of water and perhaps consider a steam sauna to humidify the vocal tract and dilute out any chlorine ions that you may have inhaled.

Am I Running my Voice into the Ground?

Dear Doctor Jahn,

I've recently become a serious runner. I've been running for years, but have begun to increase my mileage up to 25 miles per week. I'm not training for a marathon or anything; I just enjoy running. And, as my family has grown and my time has been squeezed, I find it a very efficient way to stay in shape. Is there any known effect on the voice of which I should be aware? I generally run outdoors unless it's extremely cold (well below freezing) or icy, then I stay indoors on a treadmill. Any information would be greatly appreciated. - Nathan

Dear Nathan,

As a fellow runner, I congratulate you. By all means keep it up. I think if you were to have any problems, they would have already developed, since you are doing 25 miles a week. The most important issues are catching cold and exposure to pollution and allergies. Try first of all to dress appropriately, and if you run outdoors, try to get to a warm environment soon after the run, rather than cool down completely outdoors. Also, try to breathe through your nose as much as possible: it decreases exposure to pollutants and allergens, warms the air, and helps expand the lungs due to the naso-pulmonary reflex. If it's very cold, you may consider lightly covering your face with a scarf or balaclava. If you do have allergies, don't run outdoors during allergy seasons or at times when the pollen count is high. Drink lots of water, since you lose more in sweat and exhaled vapor when running. And keep it up!

Singing Makes me Dizzy!

Dear Doctor Jahn,

Today I had a voice lesson, and I felt sick in the middle of the lesson. I felt I was going to pass out, couldn't continue singing, so I had to go home. I wasn't sure what it was, because I had never had such a symptom. Now I am thinking it might have been from singing. I was dizzy and felt like [I was] lacking oxygen. I told my husband, who is a singer, and he said he has seen a few students get dizzy when they were singing. Do you know WHY this happens? - Frankie

Dear Frankie,

The most likely cause for your dizziness is that you were hyperventilating. When you do this, you blow off too much carbon dioxide, which changes the chemistry of the fluid around the brain. Try taking somewhat shallower breaths—more specifically, don't exhale to the absolute limit when you breathe out. Incidentally, you can prove to yourself whether this is the cause of your symptoms by purposely hyperventilating: take 20 deep, full breaths rapidly, in and out, and see whether the dizziness you feel is similar to what you experience while singing. If it is, you need to change your breathing technique. Since breathing during singing usually involves a quick inhalation and slow exhalation, it would seem unlikely that you would blow off too much CO_2 during singing, but you can see if hyperventilating on purpose reproduces your symptoms.

Will Drastic Dieting Starve My Voice?

Dear Doctor Jahn,

I am a 29-year -old singer in my third year of voice studies. I will be taking part in a physician-supervised diet at a hospital. I currently weigh 260 pounds and will be fasting with liquids for 3 weeks and then moving on to an all protein diet/fast. The fast will also include a regular exercise routine of walking, cycling and some swimming. Will this rapid weight loss adversely affect my singing? - Josie

Dear Josie,

I congratulate you on this difficult undertaking. From the point of view of your general health, longevity, and even vocal longevity, you are doing the right thing. I hope you succeed in taking it off and keeping it off. In terms of the voice, a rapid loss of weight will likely have some effect. You may be low on energy. Also, the color of the voice may be somewhat different, since the shape of the resonators and the weight and size of the walls of the resonating compartments (like the palate and the tongue) have changed. Most significantly, with rapid weight change, your support will change. Your abdominal muscles, used to working with a greater bulk of abdominal contents, will be too lax to properly support the voice. You may run out of air and resort to compensatory muscling of the voice on the laryngeal end. Gradual weight loss, with concomitant abdominal exercises, is the best way to re-set these muscles and get them to function optimally.

I cannot predict exactly what these changes would be in your individual case, but it may be that you will have some adjustments to make, since you are used to working with your old instrument. Nonetheless, you should do this, and with some effort at listening and adjusting, you should be able to sing fine. The key is to lose the weight gradually and rework your vocal technique as you go along.

Can I Sing Well with a Hernia?

Dear Doctor Jahn,

I have recently been diagnosed with an umbilical hernia, and wonder whether I can continue to sing with this condition. Also, would having it repaired change my singing? - Tess

Dear Tess,

Hernias, in general, relate to areas of weakness, usually in the abdominal wall or its openings. Abdominal contents then pooch out through these openings. Inguinal hernias involve a bit of intestine protruding into the groin, and diaphragmatic hernias (also called hiatus hernia) mean that a bit of the lower intestine or stomach, usually in the abdomen, has been pushed up into the chest. Umbilical hernia relates to an area of weakness in the anterior abdominal wall, between the two long, strap-like anterior abdominal muscles (rectus abdominis). There is no muscle in this area, and once it has been stretched (such as by child bearing or excessive obesity), the umbilicus starts pointing out, pushed by the abdominal contents.

With small umbilical hernias, you can sing. Consider, however, that the weakness may extend not just to the area of the navel, but also to the fibrous tissue above and below it. This condition, called diastasis recti, may affect your ability to support the voice. Contracting your abdominal muscles, instead of pushing up on the diaphragm and supporting your voice, will be directed towards pushing out the weakened and herniated area, reducing vocal efficiency.

A simple option is to wear a supportive garment such as a girdle. The problem, of course, is that this constricts the entire abdomen and impairs the expansion of your abdomen in general as you breathe in. If an umbilical hernia (diastasis recti) becomes a significant problem, I would recommend that you have it repaired surgically. If you are a woman who sings, there may also be cosmetic advantages to surgery versus a girdle.

The Connection Between Thyroid Disease and Singing

Dear Doctor Jahn,

Can you please explain the effects of thyroid diseases on vocal production? - Kevin

Dear Kevin,

The thyroid gland secretes two major hormones which regulate the body's metabolism. In brief, benign thyroid disease causes either excessive or insufficient secretion of these hormones, called hyperthyroidism or hypothryroidism respectively.

Patients who are hyperthyroid are in a hypermetabolic state—they are hungry, always too warm, sweat a lot, lose weight, have abnormal periods, and their heart is also in overdrive. From the vocal point of view, the most significant problem is a vocal tremor. This is not a vibrato, but a lack of muscle control that cannot be technically corrected. The treatment is to diagnose the hyperthyroidism and then to suppress the excess secretion—either with medication that reduces the hormones or by ablating the thyroid tissue with radioisotopes and then replacing it with oral thyroid hormones.

More common, especially in middle-aged women, is hypothyroidism. This can be quite subtle in presentation and often begins with fatigue, a sensation of feeling cold all the time, and weight gain. Other symptoms are constipation, changes in the menses, and hair loss. The vocal issues here are a huskier voice and one that is unwieldy and loses flexibility and color.

Some women present with chronic hoarseness. As you see, these are all pretty nonspecific symptoms—who isn't tired all the time? But hypothyroidism should always be suspected, because it is easily corrected with oral medication.

Now, whether you are hyper- or hypothyroid, once the condition has been identified and your hormone levels restored to the correct (euthyroid) level, your voice should be fine. Neither hyper- nor hypothyroidism should cause any irreversible damage to your larynx or your voice.

Singing with an Eating Disorder

Dear Doctor Jahn,

I have a student in a group voice class who just revealed to me she is bulimic, wanting to know what effect that might have on her voice. Has there been any research on this? - Jade

Dear Jade,

I have seen several singers with bulimia. I would first suggest that your patient seek the appropriate therapy for the bulimia, i.e. the psychological issues. In terms of the voice, the only concern I would have is the effect of the recurrent vomiting of stomach contents. There might be an issue with damage to the vocal folds if the acidic gastric contents are regurgitated over the back of the larynx, with resulting hoarseness. Acid irritation to the pharynx, with reactive contraction of the pharyngeal muscles, might also elevate the vocal apparatus and result in an abnormally high laryngeal position with all of its attendant vocal problems.

Damage to the teeth has also been described, I believe by Dr. Bob Sataloff. The acid can damage the enamel and discolor and mar the frontal incisors. If your student has any other problems from bulimia, I would be interested in hearing about them.

Why is Swimming Exhausting my Voice?

Dear Doctor Jahn,

I recently have taken up swimming as a means of exercise. AFTER swimming for a couple of weeks I have noticed that by the time I'm done with my swim, my voice is really tired. Obviously I'm not yelling or even talking while I'm swimming, so I'm wondering if this has something to do with the chlorine. I feel as if I can't sing for quite a while (four or five hours) after I swim since my voice is so tired and worn. Is this something I should be overly concerned about? Is there something I can do to prevent it or make the effects less severe? - Simon

Dear Simon,

I am not sure what the association is, but I have a couple of thoughts. Chlorine could certainly be a problem, and since chlorine is broken down and evaporates more outdoors, the chlorine level is typically highest in indoor public pools. But you don't normally get chlorinated water down to your larynx or lungs, although some irritating spray or vapor may get in as you breathe through your mouth. On the other hand, you may get chlorine into your nose, and this could have a reflex effect on the vocal tract. We do know that breathing through an open nose increases the compliance of the lungs—i.e., makes them more flexible and effective. Conversely, breathing through your mouth, especially in the presence of an irritant such as chlorine, may have the opposite effect.

Another possible association could be if you strain your neck or shoulders during strokes. This might create a reflex tension in the pharynx and elevate the larynx. I would be interested to check your neck before and after swimming, to compare the position of the larynx. If the larynx is elevated, this can affect your voice, and you may need to work a bit to lower it again before singing well.

Finally, consider that you are breathing through your mouth while swimming - short, gasping breaths which are probably thoracic (chest breathing) and not abdominal- the opposite of what you normally do as you breathe for singing.

One way to determine which of the first two possibilities is the culprit would be to swim in a (non-chlorinated) lake during the summer and see how you feel.

How Do I Stamp out Sleep Apnea?

Dear Doctor Jahn,

I can't sleep and have been diagnosed with sleep apnea – now my challenge is to find a way to deal with it that doesn't affect the voice. What is your opinion?- Jenna

Dear Jenna,

Many people equate sleep apnea with snoring. They are two different conditions, but there is a significant overlap. Sleep-disordered breathing, whether snoring or OSA (obstructive sleep apnea), can certainly be due to mechanical obstruction in the upper airway, such as a deviated nasal septum or other causes of nasal congestion. Huge tonsils can also obstruct the airway, and removing them can at times relieve sleep apnea. Weight loss, in cases of marked obesity, is yet another good way to open the upper airway, since most of the tissues in this area contain fat cells, and can protrude into and obstruct the airway as you are inhaling. If all else fails, continuous positive airway pressure (CPAP) can be used to assist inhalation and displace tissues out of the airway as you inhale.

Although CPAP is considered the gold standard for treatment of obstructive sleep apnea, it does involve blowing air - often with some force - past the vocal folds at a high rate (12-16 times a minute). If it is a standard CPAP unit, consider reducing the air pressure from the therapeutic levels by 25 to 30 percent to decrease potential drying impact to the vocal folds. Otherwise, consider switching to Auto-CPAP to adjust the pressure as needed, as opposed to a constant pressure for all stages of the sleep cycle. Be sure the CPAP includes a humidifier and, in the winter, a heater. Do not use CPAP for at least 12-24 hours prior to an important performance unless it is a case of a very severe apnea.

Also look into other alternatives to treat OSA, such as an oral appliance, lifestyle changes (weight loss, reduced alcohol intake, etc.) or surgery.

5. Get a Gig Ready Voice

Can I Wake Up with a Gig-Ready Voice?

Dear Doctor Jahn,

I'd like to have a great singing voice first thing in the morning! So, what would be your ideal plan? I have to also add that pollen allergies, some late nights and * ahem * less than ideal performance venues add to my challenges! - Brad

Dear Brad,

Many singers have "morning voice", especially after a performance the night before. While some of this is unavoidable, I have several suggestions that should minimize the impairment. By way of prevention, try not to abuse your voice the night before: use good technique and minimize social voice use, saving it for your actual performance.

Minimize the use of alcohol— it has a dehydrating effect on the vocal folds, and an anaesthetic and disinhibiting effect centrally, both of which can lead to excessive trauma to the larynx.

If your performing environment is smoky or otherwise polluted, a steam inhaler in your dressing room would be useful for moistening the vocal tract between sets. You could get a "personal steamer", which covers the nose and mouth and is small and inexpensive.

Those breaks between sets are golden: guard them jealously! Rest your voice, try to minimize chatting with well-wishers, and stay in a relatively quiet setting rather than mingling with customers or fans. At the risk of having to get up at night for the bathroom, drink two large glasses of water on retiring, and keep the glass beside your bed for additional sips if you happen to wake up during the night. If you feel you have abused your larynx excessively, you may also consider taking one anti-inflammatory pill such as Ibuprofen (200 mg), provided that there are no medical contraindications to this. If you have any history of reflux, a tablespoon of antacid will minimize the risk of further irritation to the vocal tract at night.

The next morning, start with another glass of water, then take a long, hot, steamy shower, and gently begin to vocalize in the shower. Do this even before making any phone calls or engaging in any conversations. While vocalizing, concentrate on flexibility, doing some glissandos (slides) through the passaggio (the part of the voice where you transition from chest voice to head voice)— start with slides from top to bottom (easier), then from bottom to top, in a soft voice.

Don't start your warm-ups by pushing the voice (especially at the top) and never start to sing full out without warming up, especially after a "less than ideal" performance situation the night before.

Am I Losing My Upper Range?

Dear Doctor Jahn,

I'm a 40-year-old male and, after a hiatus, I've just returned to singing in bars and clubs. My upper vocal range has decreased and I experience a tight feeling in my throat. I also feel and hear a grinding on certain vowel sounds (A's and I's) the day after a gig or a particularly high-energy rehearsal. I'd like to get back to my old unencumbered singing self. Can you help? - Alan

Dear Alan,

Your history contains important clues as to where your problem lies and how to correct things. You have been away from singing for a while (months or years?), and have returned to a high-energy and vocally taxing profession. I suspect that your technique may need a tune-up! You are asking your voice to perform as it did when you were younger and singing regularly. A good teacher should be able to give you exercises to get your larynx back into shape. Trying to produce a voice with inadequate support or technical reserve means you are using more muscle tension in the laryngeal area to produce less voice. This accounts for the tight feeling you are experiencing.

By muscling the voice rather than supporting it properly, you are increasing the trauma to the vocal folds, which may result in some swelling. This swelling, in turn, would account for your difficulty with the high notes. If your "high notes" are in high chest voice rather than head voice, the friction and trauma is even greater. Finally, a 'high-energy rehearsal', to me, means a loud rehearsal charged with emotion. It is unlikely that, in the heat of the moment, you are monitoring the physical sensations involved in vocal production. It is therefore likely that you overusing and straining.

By way of treatment: see a good teacher to get you back on track. Drink plenty of water. Scrupulously monitor your voice during singing and, until you get your old voice back, perhaps adjust your repertoire to a less strenuous level.

Is it Normal to Feel Pain After Singing?

Dear Doctor Jahn,

Is getting a sore throat after singing something singers just have to live with? - Cathy

Dear Cathy,

The short answer is a resounding NO! Feeling pain in your throat or neck after singing is a warning that you are doing something that is technically not right. While some degree of general fatigue, vocal fatigue or even a little bit of hoarseness may occur – especially after strenuous singing – you really should not experience pain if you are singing correctly.

A sore throat after singing is an indication that you are singing with excessive tension, and means that the muscles in the throat, those moving the vocal folds and positioning the larynx in the neck, are straining and in a cramped state.

Compare this to clenching your fist tightly, and holding it in that position for a minute.
While intermittent contraction of any muscle (including the muscles of the throat) is natural, prolonged contraction causes pain.

But the complete answer is not that simple. While I would tell classical singers with post-singing discomfort that they are not using the correct technique and are attempting to get volume and projection from squeezing instead of supporting the voice from below, I also realize that for other genres such as rock, belt, gospel, or rhythm and blues, that squeezed and strained sound is exactly what you may be looking for.

Several years ago I was taking care of some of the cast members of Miss Saigon, who complained that the music was written so that it would be painful to sing in order to convey how the girls were suffering. I am certainly not suggesting that you sing musical theater, rock or blues in an operatic voice.

So, what is the solution? Always sing mindfully: be aware of what you are doing technically at all times. Use the pushed, squeezed, strained voice judiciously, as you would use spice in your cooking. Use it to maximal effect when necessary, but your fall-back position should always be a well-supported and unstrained voice, where power and projection come from the abdomen and chest, rather than the constrictor muscles of the pharynx and larynx. A good vocal coach should be able to teach you how to produce the sound you want with minimal strain.

Can Talking Well Improve My Singing?

Dear Doctor Jahn,

I don't want to seem like I'm paranoid but I've been wondering about how my talking affects my singing voice – specifically how I might change my talking throughout the day to improve my singing? If I talk in a higher/lower pitch can I improve my singing range?
- Geoff

Dear Geoff,

What a terrific question! Not many singers consider that their speaking voice and their singing voice both originate from the same source, the larynx. Not that it isn't obvious, but for some reason, many singers think of their singing voice as "the instrument", and consider voice rest as simply not singing. Since all voice comes from the larynx, what we do vocally when speaking on the phone, arguing at a noisy restaurant or bar, yelling, laughing and crying, definitely puts more miles on those vocal folds than actual singing.

Even more important, most of us do not speak using our schooled "professional" voice, but just blurt things out, come what may. And yet, if you apply good vocal technique to your speaking voice, you can reap benefits when you sing. You should ideally speak in a well-supported and well-projected voice. Speaking in head voice, although it sounds a little odd, is much less stressful to your larynx than in high chest voice. You should also modify your environment to decrease vocal stress: try to avoid speaking in a noisy environment if possible.

The worst example is a loud restaurant, with music throbbing, everyone yelling, and you, disinhibited and dehydrated from alcohol, pushing the voice to rise above the din. It has been shown that in a noisy environment we will naturally speak about 35 dB above background noise (called the Lombard effect). We do this automatically and unawares. If the ambient sound level is 70 dB, you can easily be putting out 105 dB of voice, only to pay the price later.

In general, speak as mindfully as you sing. Think about abdominal support, open throat resonance and projection. Stay well hydrated, minimize loud conversation in a noisy milieu, and consider speaking in head voice if possible.

How Can I Kickstart my Morning Voice?

Dear Doctor Jahn,

I often wake up with a raspy voice (due to a cold, or acid reflux, or a late night of singing), but I have to talk all day at my job. What are some exercises or tricks to help me get my raspy voice ready for the day? - Kendra

Dear Kendra,

"Morning voice" is a common complaint. Even in the absence of reflux or a cold, many of us wake up with a husky voice. And performing the night before, especially in a noisy, possibly smoky environment surely doesn't help! There are many factors to consider and incorporate into your management of "morning voice".

First, I would certainly address the issue of gastric reflux, a frequent condition where stomach contents regurgitate up into the esophagus and throat. If this is a problem for you, do the usual things: avoid irritating foods, late meals and excessive alcohol or coffee. Also take your reflux medications - such as proton pump inhibitors - regularly, and not only when you feel the reflux. Finally, you may consider adding an antacid (such as liquid Gaviscon or Maalox)—one tablespoon on going to bed.

An often-neglected cause of morning hoarseness is a dry throat secondary to nasal obstruction. Snoring is a tip-off, but even if you don't snore, you might breathe through your mouth at night. If your nose gets blocked, think about using Breathe-rite nasal strips to flare your nostrils open or having your nose examined for an anatomic obstruction (deviated septum).

If you just breathe with your mouth open for no reason, use a humidifier in your bedroom.

Consider the possibility of allergies causing nocturnal nasal obstruction. Dust, dust mites or feathers (or that cat sleeping beside you) are all possible culprits.

Dehydration of the throat is another area of concern. Limit your alcohol intake the night before, and aggressively rehydrate: drink plenty of water during your evening revels and keep a big glass of water beside your bed during the night.

Colds are often accompanied by excessive thick mucus, which worsens the hoarseness.

Wash your nose with salt water, drink plenty of water, and consider taking a decongestant. Keep in mind, however, that antihistamines (and to a lesser degree decongestants) are also drying.

Finally, in the morning- drink a big glass of water on awakening, then hop into a hot steamy shower—this should clean the junk off your vocal folds. Many singers vocalize in the morning (even if you are just going to your day job), and this might be a good routine.

Work on flexibility and range rather than your high notes: do your sirens, lip trills and other exercises to get the larynx moving. A last word: try to schedule your voice lessons or auditions for later in the day, if possible. You want them to hear your best voice, not the morning growl!

How Can I Make a Sexy Breathy Sound?

Dear Doctor Jahn,

I'm curious: I have a friend who sings in a sultry, airy voice. My voice is more clear (I think both styles are great) – but what is it, exactly, that makes her voice sound "breathy"? And could I do that??? - Ken

Dear Ken,

What an interesting question! The answer is complex, and I can only give you some medically- oriented thoughts that may be relevant. You should also speak to a good voice coach.

First, your friend is a woman, and there are some definite gender differences in what women can do vocally versus men. There are basic anatomic differences in the larynx and the preferred mode of breathing, which make it easier for women to sing "intimately". There may also be individual differences between singers of the same gender – think of Astrud Gilberto – which allow them to produce a signature voice that is difficult to duplicate. When you think, for example, about Marilyn Monroe's famous "Happy Birthday Mr. President" (or her rendition of "I Want To Be Loved By You" in the film "Some Like It Hot"), there is a breathy, sultry sexiness and intimacy that would be difficult (and inappropriate) for a male singer to reproduce.

Some of this quality comes from pushing more air past the vocal folds than you might optimally for efficient singing, whether classical or musical theater. The vocal folds are held slightly apart and of course all of this limits how loud you can sing; you are using the lungs and vocal mechanism at less than optimal efficiency in terms of clarity, projection and dynamics.

You can also change the voice by "covering", something that men can do as well as women. This means covering the top of the pharynx, usually by keeping the base of the tongue back. The effect is an intimacy, a darkness to the voice. This is used in opera (called "voix couverte"), usually when the singer shares an "aside" with the audience. When the singer says something, like voicing his inner thoughts, with the conventional understanding that the other singers on stage don't hear him, this is often done with a covered voice.

Some singers always sing with this voice, either by preference (to try to darken it) or because they cannot lower their larynx without pushing the entire tongue-hyoid complex back also.

In musical theater, this effect is often used to convey intimacy, a sense of "I am singing only to you" – Mandy Patinkin is one performer who comes to mind. But this effect, like most, is most convincing when used intermittently, rather than as your baseline singing voice.

Apart from the above, changing the shape of the resonators (pharynx, mouth) as well as the position and shape of the tongue, all influence your voice. Keep in mind, also, that in certain genres, like jazz, blues and musical theater, it is easier to use this kind of voice.

And finally: there may be abnormalities in the larynx that can make the voice sound more diffuse, husky/sexy and project an air of intimacy. Vocal fold nodules, chronic swelling of the vocal folds (the "cigarettes-whiskey-and-midnight voice"), post-menopausal changes – all of these can make the voice breathier, lower, darker, and produce an impression of heightened intimacy, urgency, and personal communication.

How Can I Make My Morning Voice Remain?

Dear Doctor Jahn,

My career is just starting to take off but I have to admit that my voice only sounds the way I want it to for the first 30 minutes in the morning! It is very pliable, unique, a but raspy and powerful. This "magic" will only last until my voice gets warmed up, and once it does, I lose the biting and unique sound, and it becomes weak, less pliable and has much more "breaks". What is happening in the morning, and is there a way to sustain this voice for performances? - Tim

Dear Tim,

I read your question with interest – most singers dislike their "morning voice", and are often apologetic during a morning visit to my office if I ask them to vocalize. So the question really has two aspects: what makes your voice different in the morning from later in the day; but, equally important, what is your idea of a good voice? I ask this because for some types of singing, raspy husky or lower tone is considered better, whereas the warmed up voice, which is centered at a higher pitch and may be clearer, is not what is called for.

Consider that during the night, your vocal folds are at rest – not completely immobile, since they gently open and close with each breath, but certainly not moving significantly.

Consider also that they may dry out a bit: you don't swallow while asleep, you don't drink water, and you may breathe through your mouth. The surface of the folds can then be dry. Further, if you have reflux while sleeping, the larynx may be come elevated, and even a bit inflamed, resulting in edema and a temporary thickening of the tissues. When you phonate with such vocal folds, you need to muscle the voice a bit more, which also changes the quality.

Any of these phenomena can explain what you describe, although I can't honestly explain the pliability – most singers find that pliability increases as they warm up, especially in the mix.

Now: how to hang on to this voice? I would suggest that you go to a good voice coach and demonstrate the two voices to him/her, to see if you can learn to mimic that morning voice any time of the day, with good technique to preserve your larynx.

My Voice is Getting Old – Can I Wind Back the Clock?

Dear Doctor Jahn,

I am a man in my late forties and sing mostly rock. After a few years away from singing, I have come back to it, and I am finding my voice seems to have changed. My falsetto is almost gone and my range has shrunk. Is this due to aging or just the hiatus from singing? How does aging affect the voice? - Alexander

Dear Alexander,

There are many aspects to your question that we need to consider, and I will try to make this brief - it could take up many pages. First, the late 40s is not old from the vocal point of view, especially for men who don't need to deal with impending menopause. Many rock singers perform well into their 50s and even 60s. Here are some questions for you to consider:

1) Are you a trained singer? If you had good fundamental vocal training, especially if you had some classical training, it will be

easier to regain your voice. If, on the other extreme, you had no training and got by on talent, will power and raw muscle, you will have some difficulties regaining your 20-year-old throat. Either way, I would suggest some lessons to rediscover and rework your instrument before getting out on stage.

2) Have you led a healthy or physically demanding life? Singing does not only depend on your vocal folds, but also your lungs, abdominal support, and general state of health. What else have your vocal cords been doing these last 20 years? What is your day job, how is your social life? Wear and tear occurs whether you're singing, using your voice at work, or ordering a drink at noisy bar. Chronologic age is probably less important in this regard than biologic age.

3) Have you considered working back into your repertoire slowly, not suddenly? Start with songs that are less demanding to reacquaint your vocal mechanism (including your brain) with singing. Singing is not just about vocal cords. If, after all of the above, you're still having problems, have your larynx examined. If your falsetto is gone, there may be structural changes that need to be examined by a doctor.

4) Have you considered a slight change in repertoire or transposing some keys? Many good singers continue to sing well even in later years with the help of transposition: if you look at YouTube performances of Johnny Mathis doing the great ballad "Chances Are" in later years, you'll find that he has transposed it down about a third, but is still singing it well.

Can I Body-Build my Voice Muscles?

Dear Doctor Jahn,

I have been told that the larynx is a muscle like other muscles and I just need to work it hard to get a stronger voice. Is this true?' - Millie

Dear Millie,

Over the years I have seen many singers who habitually over-practice. They are usually serious and driven students, and typically they develop vocal problems: swelling of the vocal folds and sometimes small nodes, along with other signs of excessive muscle engagement such as elevation of the larynx with excess tension in the area of the larynx above the vocal folds. The voice often sounds muscled, the vibrato tight, the singing effortful. The contraction of the supraglottic resonating space reduces the loudness and the ring in the voice. When I ask some of these patients about their practice habits, they proudly tell me that they sing many hours—up to six or more every day. And now, they're in trouble.

To practice optimally, we need to consider what the learning process involves. While there is no doubt that years of practicing and performing brings about physical changes in the vocal tract —just palpate the abdomen of any well-trained singer—building singing muscles is not the aim of practicing.

Learning to sing, like acquiring any other skill, is primarily a mental process. Becoming aware of and gaining conscious control over normally reflexive movements takes place in the mind. Mindful control is involved in learning to raise and lower the larynx, integrating sound, proprioception, position sensation, coordinating breath and voice . . . and the list goes on. These are all abilities that involve training the brain and not the muscle. So, rather than endless repetition, the key to successful practice lies in the ability to focus; to single-mindedly concentrate.

The larynx is not a muscle that can simply be strengthened as one might do with repetitive exercises at the gym, and a "muscular" larynx (if there were such a thing) would not necessarily be a better larynx, as a biceps might be. Rather, it is a delicate and composite structure whose function, both respiratory and vocal, depends not so much on strength as on responsiveness and coordination.

Furthermore, there is a physical limit to how much mechanical trauma the vocal folds can take. Over-singing, whether in practice or in performance, can damage the larynx. So, unlike piano practice, which can go on for many hours at a time, vocal practice needs to be better, not more. While you have no control over the length of a Wagner opera, you do over your daily practice. It needn't be long as much as meaningful: you need to extract every bit of gain from every minute of singing, and feed that information to train your central nervous system.

Why? Because the brain is where learning takes place. Anatomically and physiologically, this process takes many forms. During practice, central nervous connections are constantly rewired and potential pathways activated. There is now evidence that listening to sounds not only opens new nervous pathways in the brain but can actually (at least in experimental young animals) cause new neurons to grow. Furthermore, these neurons are tonotopic. That is, they are selectively responsive to the specific sound frequency that caused them to form.

Memorizing music, like memorizing anything, initially involves electric storage of information (somewhat like a battery stores charge) and, eventually, the synthesis of proteins—both brain activities. Hearing music or seeing a performance activates mirror neurons in the brain, which prepare you to sing and perform yourself, and to vicariously experience the event. So, although singing a long piece or role obviously requires stamina and repetitive run-throughs, the real learning is about intensity rather than length. Optimizing your practice therefore means making use of every repetition, and everything else you do during practice, to stimulate the brain. And this requires constant awareness and attention.

One way to improve your yield from practicing is by developing concentration in other ways. Yoga, meditation, visualization, Qi Gong and Tai Chi are some of the techniques that you might use to train yourself to focus on specific areas and, at the same time, to disregard distracting and competing external stimuli and mind noise.

Ask yourself: What am I trying to achieve from today's practice? Are you learning new music? A great deal of music can, and should, be learned and memorized without singing or playing a single note. Even muscle memory originates in the central nervous system, although not in the conscious cortex. The great German pianist Walter Gieseking was renowned for his concentration and could commit music to memory without ever touching the keyboard. He was able, so the story goes, to learn an entire program by just looking at the music and analyzing—all this while sitting on the train, travelling from one concert hall to the next.

On the other hand, if the purpose of your practice is to test your stamina to get through an entire performance (whether a long set, a recital or even an opera), that will obviously require a different sort of practice. You just need to be clear at the onset about what the purpose of your practice is.

You might test the quality of your practice by playing a little game. Imagine that you were allowed a limited time to practice, say 20 minutes a day. How would you change what you do in order to suck every bit of learning out of your practice during this time? You would set concrete goals, prioritize, and fully engage— physically and mentally—in the moment. Distractions, both external and internal, would fade away. The ability to be intensely and consistently "in the moment" will maximally engage your brain and improve the value of your practice.

And the habit of mindfulness, once acquired, can then extend to and enrich every aspect of your daily life. A famous Chinese story tells of a young Buddhist monk who, after joining a monastery, requests permission to speak with the abbot, a wise old man. Bowing, he asks, "Master, how do I attain enlightenment?" The abbot looks up, points to a broom in the corner of the room, and says, simply, "Sweep the floor."

Mindfulness - being fully aware and in the moment - is the key, whether you're practicing, performing, eating your dinner or sweeping the floor. Being fully engaged, body and mind, wholly in the present, will not only maximize the benefits you derive from vocal practice but will enlighten everything you do, as a singer and as a sentient human being.

What Do the False Folds Do?

Dear Doctor Jahn,

I think I just barely understand that much of my voice is created by my vocal folds – two little eensy weeny flaps of flesh down my throat somewhere. OK. Check. But then someone mentioned that I should know about the "false folds" Huh??? This is getting weird and complicated. Help! - Kal

Dear Kal,

I'm glad you are interested in the anatomy of the larynx, which can be a bit complex. Here is "the short version"; a longer version is available in our book, *The Singer's Guide to Complete Health* (Oxford University Press, 2013).

The vocal folds are two bands of tissue that run front to back, like two elastic bands. Air flows between them as you exhale. If they are approximated in the midline and you continue to push air, they begin to vibrate and generate sound. The sound then resonates in the spaces in your throat, above the vocal folds.

Above the vocal folds are two other folds of tissue which do not normally vibrate. This is because they are pulled out of the air stream, and are also made of thicker tissue.

These folds, the false vocal cords, are, in reality, one of three safeguards for the airway: when you swallow or choke, they squeeze together to prevent material from being inhaled into the lungs.

They normally do not vibrate and have no role in singing, but it gets more complicated. There are some people who squeeze the false folds together when they speak or sing. By doing this, they put them in the way of the exhaled stream of air, and can actually produce sound with them. It is a rough, gravelly sound, exemplified by singers such as Louis Armstrong, and not normal for most types of singing.

So for your purposes, I would ignore them. If you do use them to "sing" (known as "false cord phonation"), your listeners will probably not thank you...

What Should my Tongue Be Doing When I'm Singing?

Dear Doctor Jahn,

Someone just told me that I have to relax my tongue when I sing. I've been reading for a couple of years and I think I understand that my throat and neck should be relaxed – so what is the deal with the tongue? - Hannah

Dear Hannah,

I will answer this based on what I know medically, but you may also want to direct this question to a good vocal coach for an answer from the technical perspective.

The tongue is a large muscle - actually a complex set of muscles - that allow the tongue to move in any direction and assume many different shapes and positions in the mouth. When the muscles tense, at least three things happen that can affect singing negatively.

First, the increase in muscle tone causes a reflexive increase in muscle tone in neighboring muscles, including those of the jaw, neck and the larynx. In neurology, this phenomenon is called "reinforcement". This increase in tone means you are singing with greater tension and more effort. Increasing muscle tone in the vocal muscles specifically raises the larynx, tilts it forward, creates a posterior gap between the vocal folds, and reduces the resonating space above the vocal folds. The voice sounds muscled, thinner and less resonant.

Second, when the muscles of the tongue contract, the tongue bunches up, particularly in the back. It looks like a big lump or ball. One of the tricks singers need to learn is to keep the back of the tongue flat against the floor of the mouth. This opens the oropharynx and allows the voice to come forward, rather than covering it in the back. It also increases the size of the resonating space in the back of the mouth.

Finally, a tense tongue is less flexible and agile, and this may impact your articulation, especially for consonants that require tongue tip mobility. But most important is really the first point: uncontrolled and purposeless tension anywhere in the vocal tract causes reflexive tightening and harmful muscle effort in other parts of the vocal tract.

Can You Solve My Mysterious Throat Pain?

Dear Doctor Jahn,

Have you ever heard of a singer having what seems to be muscular pain in the back/top of the throat after singing? It's as if the soft palate itself (or the back of the tongue, or both) has somehow been strained. Is that even possible? ENTs have assured [me] that there is no laryngitis, reflux, or pathological considerations present. Also, I am not a belter. A stroboscopy looks normal. Where is the pain coming from? I'd be very grateful for your insight, even your guesses and possibilities! - Nina

Dear Nina,

Since your ENT exam was normal, I would assume that the palate is moving symmetrically and well, and that you have no problems with changes in the nasality of your voice (either more nasal or less nasal). So, it sounds like muscle strain. Possible causes might be: new repertoire, a change of performance schedule or venue, a new teacher or new technique. Are you singing more now, or in a performance space where you need to push the voice more (longer performances, louder accompaniment, etc.)? A neuromuscular problem is much less likely, but if you get other muscle pains or fatigue, you should see a neurologist.

What's Happening Inside My Breathy Tone?

Dear Doctor Jahn,

I am trying to get that 'breathy tone' on a few of my songs – even to the point where I go to a whisper. I am just wondering what is actually going on with my voice when I do this? - Polly

Dear Polly,

The vocal folds do not only come together with phonation or singing. They also approximate with whistling, pushing and whispering, and generally move back and forth during normal respiration. There are two kinds of whisper, the voiced and unvoiced. The unvoiced whisper is barely audible and is not generally used. It involves almost unrestricted airflow through the larynx. The voiced whisper does involve some vibration of the vocal folds or other laryngeal structures, and can be soft, stronger (like a stage whisper), and even a whisper-like singing voice, as you mentioned. In these cases, the vocal folds are held firmly by the laryngeal muscles, although they do not completely approximate, at least not along their entire length. In terms of muscle effort, this sort of whisper is definitely more tiring than well supported singing or speaking. Breathy singing usually involves strong muscular effort pushing the vocal folds together, but leaving a gap, usually posteriorly. This is very effortful, involves high laryngeal tension, and can, in the long run, lead to nodules. It is also a less effective way of using the breathing mechanism, since you use more air to produce a voice (some of it "spilled" between the open vocal folds).

At What Age is a Voice Fully Grown?

Dear Doctor Jahn,

How long will a young woman's voice continue to grow? What are the factors affecting how big a voice will get? My daughter is just a few months shy of 15. She has a fairly large and well-developed voice for a 15-year-old. But we have been told that because of her petite, slender 5'1" frame that her voice will probably not get large enough to be very competitive after the age of 18. What are your thoughts on this? - Martha

Dear Martha,

A number of factors can affect how long a young woman's voice continues to grow - some developmental and some technical. Developmentally, the voice will continue to grow for some time after menarche, and the best rough guide to whether she is "fully grown" would likely be bone age, which can be estimated with a simple X-ray to look at the epiphyses (the ends of the bones of the hand). Of course, a fully-grown young woman can be petite and slim, or tall, or more robust in size. The best indicator would be to look at the parents.

Typically, teenagers grow in their trunk and extremities first, and the head assumes its adult dimensions last. Since the size and resonance of the voice relates not only to the size of the thorax (trunk) but also to the length of the vocal folds and the size of the resonating cavities above them, full growth can take several years.

Now, the technical side: while the voice may be fully developed in terms of its anatomical underpinnings (i.e. lungs and vocal folds) at a relatively young age, it can continue to change in range and color for many years during a singer's development. Power and projection can also develop as technique is acquired. But each voice is different: like wine, it can be fresh and fully developed early, or can take many years to mature and unfold.

May I just add one comment regarding your qualifier "to be competitive"? While I understand that it is a highly competitive world out there, the only challenge for every singer is to reach his or her maximum capability. How that measures up with the competition is important, but cannot be the primary goal. Singers who work to achieve an arbitrary external (rather than internal) standard may over sing and extend themselves beyond their limit, which will eventually lead to vocal difficulties.

How Can I Get Rid of Habitual Jaw Tension?

Dear Doctor Jahn,

I have a terrible habit of biting my lip. I know it sounds very minor, but I've been doing it for about 20 years now – I'm 25 – and my jaw is constantly tight and sore from the pressure of biting down on my lip. What can I do to stop this? I'm afraid it will affect my singing in the long run if I'm always clenching my jaw. Any suggestions?
- Lucy

Dear Lucy,

Habits like this are very difficult to break. Some people habitually bite the inside of their cheek, and actually develop little fibromas along the bite line. I have a couple of suggestions. If you do clench your teeth, especially at night, you may ask your dentist to make a bite block. This is a clear acrylic cover that goes over your lower teeth and reduces clenching. It may also remind you not to bite your lip. Physical therapy to the jaw muscles and TM joint can also loosen things up. Lastly, botulinum toxin (Botox) injections are available for TMJ dysfunction: the medication is injected into the jaw muscle to reduce the pressure on the TM joint by slightly weakening the masseter muscles. This is not yet widely available as treatment, but it may be useful - not for stopping the lip biting, but for reducing resultant jaw tension.

6. Travel in Style

How Can I Have a Healthy Tour?

Dear Doctor Jahn,

I'm about to go touring...again. It's on a bus across the country. Last year, it was a heck of a lot of fun, but I was plagued with low-grade infections which led to less than ideal performances. I don't smoke (though I'm around it!) and don't drink too, too much. I'm just wondering what advice do you have for me to be the healthiest I can be on this year's trip? - Jack

Dear Jack,

Touring is difficult, both for your voice and your general health. There are many reasons. The schedule can be hectic - arriving, unpacking, rehearsing, performing and packing up again. It is stressful to deal day after day with new circumstances, different venues and different people. You are constantly in a noisy environment, since even on the bus the ambient noise level is significant and can lead to voice strain.

Depending on your group's smoking policy, your bus may be a travelling gas chamber, filled with second hand smoke that is irritating to your throat. Stress relief often takes the form of parties, which are also noisy, smoky, and not good for your vocal tract.

First, get a good set of ear-plugs, or - if you can afford them - noise cancellation head phones. Bose makes a rather expensive pair, but cheaper ones are also available; just reducing the ambient noise level on the bus goes a long way towards allowing you and your throat to relax. You can attach the phones to your iPod or CD player and replace stress-inducing traffic noise with quiet music.

Next, try to prevail on the tour manager to get rid of smoking, or at least banish it to the back of the bus. Limit second hand smoke irritation by breathing through your nose (not your mouth) and use saline nasal spray frequently, to help trap smoke particles in the nasal tract.

Drink lots of water on the bus (you may need to sit near the toilet, but that is a small price to pay). Also, have a routine that you adhere to daily. It should include some quiet time, even if just going for a short walk in a park or wooded area. If your hotel has a gym, try to use it - exercise is great stress relief.

If you know how to meditate, a few minutes daily can be very refreshing and balancing.

At the risk of being anti-social, don't be the life of every post-performance cast party. Your voice is your living, so don't waste it on things you don't get paid for. This is especially important for shows where the roles are not covered: the show and the rest of the cast depend on you being healthy and strong.

Try to eat well, not out of machines back stage. A few years ago, while touring with the Metropolitan Opera in Japan, I noticed that many musicians were eating out of the machines, which were filled with high sodium noodle soups. These are not only lacking nutrition, but also can increase high blood pressure.

Try to pick up fresh fruit and produce whenever possible. Depending on the safety of the local water supply, you may need to peel this before you eat. If you get comfort from certain foods, try to make them part of your routine; a morning bowl of oatmeal, perhaps with fruits or nuts, is a very healthy anchor to your daily menu.

Take dietary supplements, especially Vitamin C, spaced over the course of the day. Before leaving on tour, consider going to your doctor to pick up emergency drugs, such as a course of antibiotics, just in case.

Finally, call home! Some of the stress of touring comes from losing contact with your family. If you can, call or e-mail regularly to keep yourself emotionally connected during your travels. Skype, if available, is a comforting anchor which keeps you in touch with your loved ones.

I'm Going Mad with a Blocked Ear!

Dear Doctor Jahn,

It's been months and one of my ears never "popped" clear after a flight! To make things worse, when I sing it sounds like I'm wearing earplugs. I've had scans etc. and there appears to be nothing wrong. There's no allergies or anything else I can think of – help! Those who have to listen to my singing beg you! - Rob

Dear Rob,

It sounds like the problem is with your Eustachian tube, the passage that connects the middle ear to the back of your throat.

Two possibilities come to mind. More commonly, the tube gets blocked. This can be due to inflammation, allergies, or tissue (like adenoids) blocking the end of the tube in the back of the throat. Your ENT doctor should be able to determine any of these possibilities by looking in the back of your nose, looking at your eardrum, and then testing the middle ear pressure (tympanogram).

Less common, and often missed, is a Eustachian tube that is abnormally OPEN. This condition (patulous Eustachian tube) is confusing, because the symptoms are a bit like the closed tube.

The ear feels blocked. Typically, these patients say the voice echoes up into the ear, and, classically, you feel better when you are lying down than when you have been up and about all day. Also, it is worse when the adrenaline is pumping, such as with exercise or performing. Weight loss also predisposes to this condition.

You need to see another ENT and have them test your Eustachian tube for abnormal patency. If you do have this, one option is a little weight gain; another might be the placement of a small vent tube in your ear drum.

Can I Shield my Voice from a Smoky Environment?

Dear Doctor Jahn,

Is there any way to protect the voice in smoky bars? You see, I often perform in smoky places such as bars. I was wondering, what steps I can take to protect my voice, and to help me perform my best in such smoky situations?
- Ray

Dear Ray,

The problem you describe used to be much more common before the increasingly universal smoking ban was introduced in North America, as well as in many parts of Europe. Nonetheless, smoking continues, often in confined and poorly ventilated venues.

Most singers who believe they are "allergic to tobacco" are not so much allergic as just irritated in their upper respiratory tract from inhaled second-hand smoke.

Short of posting a prominent "Do Not Smoke" sign, there are several measures you can take to reduce any irritation or damage to the voice from smoky performing environments. First, try to breathe through your nose as much as possible. Obviously, when you sing or speak, you will preferentially inhale through your mouth, so unless you need to mingle with the customers, try to limit your non-singing vocal activities. If you have a quieter dressing room where you can retire between sets, do so—and while there, drink some water!

Second, use a saline nasal spray frequently between sets. This moisturizes the nasal lining and helps trap irritating particles in the nasal mucus before they reach your larynx.

Next, stay well hydrated: drink lots of water to moisturize your pharyngeal and laryngeal mucous membranes; this also helps to clear out inhaled debris. Limit your alcohol intake, since alcohol dehydrates you, and, along with loud social speaking and singing, increases possible damage to the throat (have you ever been to a quiet bar?).

Finally, you may consider inhaling some steam at the end of your evening, either from a vaporizer or as part of a long hot shower. This, again, wets the mucous membranes, and allows the little hairs (cilia) to work more effectively to clear out any inhaled debris.

And, it goes without saying: don't hang out at the stage door with the smokers!

The Nevada Desert is Drying Out my Voice!

Dear Doctor Jahn,

Do you have a recommended regimen for singers performing in arid climates? Twice while performing in the desert, I had situations where my upper register stopped phonating and squeaked. I was sleeping with a humidifier in my room, drinking over a gallon of water a day, and even tried taking Mucinex. Nothing seemed to help me regain a feeling of being hydrated. I am scheduled to perform in Las Vegas soon, and want to have this problem tackled by then. - Heidi

Dear Heidi,

This is a real problem. I remember several years ago one of my New York patients was singing with the Santa Fe Opera and, in addition to the three-hour time change, also had to battle the dryness of the air. I have a few thoughts for you.

First, continue your increased water intake. I would suggest 8-10 glasses a day, if your stomach and bladder can handle that. If you exercise, don't forget to replace sweat with additional water.

Second, use saline nasal spray frequently. Since you normally breathe through your nose (although not while singing), you should take advantage of the humidifying ability of the nasal turbinates (these are shelves of tissue that run the length of the nose and warm and moisten the inhaled air). Social talking usually is also associated with mouth breathing, so monitor this.

Third, minimize taking substances that can dry your mucous membranes. This includes alcohol, antihistamines, and any other medication that you don't have to take. (Many drugs, such as antidepressants and the diuretics you might take for blood pressure, are also drying). Spend time in the shower or steam sauna if these are available to you.

And finally, you should think about getting some saline right down into the throat, using an atomizer spray, a steamer, or a nebulizer. Be sure, however, that you use only sterile "normal" (a.k.a. "physiologic") saline, which is 0.9 percent sodium chloride. You can buy this in bottles at the drug store.

How Can I Find Vocal Power on Tour?

Dear Doctor Jahn,

I'm just about to embark on a major European tour (2 gigs a day, seven days a week for 5 weeks) and I don't want my voice to fail! I'm open to any advice! - Gary

Dear Gary,

Touring can be stressful to your body on many levels, and before we talk about your singing, consider that the voice is only as healthy as you are. So in general, try to drink a lot of water, rest, eat well and take your vitamins!

The voice – your voice – will need to work hard, and under a variety of circumstances, some of which you cannot control. My most important advice is: save your voice for when you need it.

Minimize social voice use, especially between and after your performances – give it a chance to recover between performances. Avoid noisy places if you can, since the tendency there is to raise your voice above the background din. If a noisy environment is unavoidable (such as an airplane, car or tour bus), keep your mouth shut. Noise tends to tense the larynx. If your tour involves a lot of one-nighters with travel in between, noise cancellation headphones are a good investment.

If you stay at better hotels, make use of the gym (hopefully one without loud music) and sauna to stretch and relax. In general, try to plan your day's activities around your performances, and keep in mind that you have only one larynx, whether it is singing, talking on the bus or yelling at the pub.

During performances, make sure the sound system is working to your advantage. You should not need to strain to be heard. If you work with the same sound crew throughout your tour, make sure they are sensitive to your needs. If you need to work with different people, the sound check is even more important. If ear level monitors are an option, these can also help to reduce vocal strain during performance.

After the show, relax - but not in a noisy venue. Drink water before, during and after your performance. Well-hydrated vocal folds will better tolerate trauma than dehydrated ones.

Finally, the more you can adhere to a comfortable routine, the better. Unexpected stress weakens your immune system, and you will be in contact with many different people (some inevitably suffering from colds), so keeping your immune system strong is key.

How Can I Cure Blocked Ears When Flying?

Dear Doctor Jahn,

I just got back from a gig in Sedona and I cannot get my right ear to regulate. This happens whenever I fly (I usually try to travel by train). I've been given the remedy of washing out my ears with one-part alcohol and one-part white vinegar — does this do any damage? I'm seeing an acupuncturist

tonight to help me with my chronic back pain – will this help me with releasing the pressure in my ears? - Brian

Dear Brian,

You most likely have a blocked Eustachian tube, which can happen when you fly with a cold, allergy or congestion. Normally, as the ambient air pressure changes with airplane ascent (and especially descent), the pressure spontaneously equalizes between the back of the throat and the middle ear through the Eustachian tube. When the tube or the nasopharynx (the part of the pharynx above the palate and behind the nose) are congested, the pressure cannot equalize.

You may then notice discomfort in the ear, with a sense of blockage or hearing loss. In severe cases, you might even develop some fluid in the middle ear that may require drainage.

Try to open the Eustachian tube by using a decongestant, either oral (such as Pseudoephedrine – also known as PSE) or a nasal spray (such as oxymetazoline), and popping your ears. If you are seeing an acupuncturist, have her/him stimulate the "nasopharynx" point just inside your ear canal – this often releases the blockage.

If the problem is indeed due to blocked Eustachian tubes, washing your ears with vinegar will not help. However, acupuncture can be useful, particularly ear acupuncture. The "Eustachian tube" or "rhinopharynx" point on the external ear should be needled, and this can often release Eustachian tube blockage.

What's The Best Way to Medicate Travel Sickness?

Dear Doctor Jahn,

When I fly, especially on smaller planes, nausea and vomiting are an absolute certainty. I normally take Dramamine, which works quite well, but it dries me out and makes me sleepy. Normally this isn't an issue, but now that my calendar is starting to fill up, I suddenly find myself needing another option. I have a performance on Friday in one city, and on Saturday in another, which means I will have to sing shortly after getting off of the plane. What medication do you suggest as an alternative for a singer who suffers from motion sickness and must perform shortly after, or the day after, plane travel?
- Naomi

Dear Naomi,

Unfortunately, most anti-nausea medications are in the antihistamine family, and are therefore drying. I have a couple of suggestions, though. You could take some ginger capsules or candied ginger; both are good traditional remedies for nausea. There are also a couple of good acupuncture points for nausea on the forearm (also one on the ear). You should consider getting an anti-motion sickness wristband, which puts pressure on one of these points and might help you avoid throwing up. If you can find a good ear acupuncturist, they can implant a small stud into the ear's acupuncture point (like the ones they use for weight loss or anti-smoking). Rubbing this during the flight might decrease your nausea.

You could also try some Valium, a drug that I sometimes give for vertigo. It is less drying than Antivert, Dramamine, or Bonine. If you absolutely need to take a Dramamine-type medication, drink as much water as you can—not huge quantities at once, but small sips throughout the flight. Cold water (or even ice chips) is better than warm drinks, in terms of nausea.

Finally, if the flight is a longer one, such as overseas, you might try a sleeping pill like Ambien. It is less drying, and if you are asleep you may not get nauseous.

Flying Without Mucus

Dear Doctor Jahn,

Whenever I travel, usually to a gig, I find that I need at least two days to recover from the airplane experience, a luxury I can't afford. I attribute my problems to thick and mostly dry mucus from dehydration on the plane - my voice feels like it's "stuck in the mud." I take Mucinex (guaifenesin), humidify at night, and drink water until I can't stand it. Is there anything else I can do? - Ian

Dear Ian,

Here are a couple of thoughts: inhale steam when you arrive—either from a personal steamer or a shower. Drink lots of water before, during, and after the flight. Spray Ayr Saline Nasal Gel spray into your nose on the plane; this should coat your mucous membranes and reduce drying. Also, wash your nose with a Neti pot, using a half-and-half saline and Alkalol (NOT alcohol!) mixture, which also dissolves mucus. Avoid talking excessively on the plane, breathe through your nose, and don't drink alcohol on the flight.

7. To Medicate or Not Medicate?

What's the Truth About Menthol Lozenges?

Dear Doctor Jahn,

I have had lots of pollen allergies and find that the resulting "gunk" is best dealt with by sucking on Hall's Mentho-lyptus lozenges. Are they harmful? If so, could you recommend a lozenge that would break up the gunk equally well yet not be harmful? What do you recommend for chronic allergy problems such as mine?
- Pierre

The short answer to your question, Pierre, is that Mentho-lyptus is not an anaesthetic, although too much menthol can be an irritant, certainly if it is inhaled. You have had no problems with it so far, and I see no reason to stop using it, unless you're concerned about exposing your teeth to a chronic sugary environment. The more complete answer to your problem would be that you should have skin testing for allergies to find out what you may be allergic to, and if necessary begin desensitization treatments. If the allergies are to inhalants (pollen, spores), ask the allergist about how to minimize exposure (such as avoiding outdoors activities at certain times of day, using air purifiers, etc.) and use lots of saline spray in your nose to wash away pollen.

Higher voices, especially in the higher range, are more critically affected by allergies and anything else that increases swelling or mucus on the vocal folds. Drink 8-10 glasses of water a day to thin this out. Some patients have had good experience with slippery elm lozenges to thin the mucus, and one voice teacher has used the dietary supplement L-cysteine with good effect. I have no personal experience with this orally ingested L-cysteine. Acetyl-cysteine is available in the US only as a nebulizer to break up thick mucous plugs for serious pulmonary problems such as cystic fibrosis; however, it is available in Europe as a dissolving tablet which can be taken with water.

No Medication Can Beat my Phlegm!

Dear Doctor Jahn,

I have had problems with excess phlegm for several years now, and this has made it very difficult for me to count on my voice being there consistently. I have taken countless antibiotics and steroids, plus nasal sprays such as Flonase and Atrovent. I have tried reflux medication and been tested for allergies, the latter being the standard tests, all of which have come up negative. Since I have tested negative for allergies, my ENT has now suggested" non-allergic rhinitis". I would appreciate any ideas that you might care to share. - Zack

Thank you for your question, Zack. In brief, my recommendations for your problem would be the following:

1) Get tested for FOOD allergies

2) Go on a non-dairy diet

3) Get tested for thyroid function

4) Drink 8-10 glasses of water a day

5) Try mucus thinners

6) Consider washing your nose with saline and steroid. You will need a prescription for Pulmocort Respule from your doctor - this is dissolved in saline.

If you have colleagues who sing in Europe or Israel, have them bring back acetyl cysteine, which is available in those countries (not in the USA) as an effervescent tablet. This breaks up mucus quite effectively. Let me know how you make out.

Hemorrhoid Cream for the Voice – Cure or Quackery?

Dear Doctor Jahn,

I heard a coach say that you can apply an anti-inflammatory ointment such as a hemorrhoid cream right on the outside of your throat at your larynx and this will reduce vocal fold swelling! Can this be true?
- Allan

Dear Allan,

Although this is incorrect, it is not as bizarre as it sounds at first. Hemorrhoid remedies such as Preparation H contain witch hazel, which is an astringent. This means that it reduces inflammation and swollen tissue.

Preparation H has been used by plastic surgeons as a cream to apply over the face to reduce inflammation, and Tucks, which is a moistened towelette used for inflamed hemorrhoids, has been used by some to reduce swelling of the eye lids.

Here is the problem, however. Laryngitis, or swelling of the vocal folds, is an internal problem, at some distance from the surface skin covering the neck. There is no anatomic way that applying an astringent to the outside of your neck will reduce internal inflammation of the larynx. Unless there is some indirect effect, such as a reflex or shared innervation, that most of us are not aware of, I would have to disagree with your coach.

Will Attention Deficit Disorder Meds Rattle my Voice?

Dear Doctor Jahn,

I am a high school junior studying to be a singer and I have ADD. I have been tested, so I know for a fact that my inability to focus is legit, and I'm trying to find a medication that could help me focus to improve my grades and focus on my music (I have until this point been dealing with it without medication). That having been said, what potential effect could medications such as Adderall have on the voice? - Joe

Dear Joe,

In my experience, you should not have any difficulties. Other laryngologists have reported a tremor that may develop in the voice. As with so many other medications, how you as an individual respond is rather idiosyncratic. I would suggest you try the drug and see how it affects you. There are other ADD drugs on the market, so you and your doctor can try various ones to find the one with maximum benefit and minimum downside.

Do Nasal Sprays Have Long Term Side Effects?

Dear Doctor Jahn,

More and more singers seem to be relying on cortisone nasal sprays and injections to mask illness symptoms in order to avoid cancelling performances when ill with sore throats, sinusitis, or the flu. Could you address the long- and short-term side effects of the use of these medications and explain the dangers of relying on these drugs for singing? I would like to make my colleagues more aware of the negative aspects of this use that exceeds the loss of an evening's pay check, as well as inform the beginning singers who are easily encouraged to depend on medicine to replace technique and discipline. - Karly

Dear Karly,

First, I share your concern for singers who deal with chronic problems by simply relying on cortisone from one concert to another. This is really a topic for an entire column, because it touches so many areas—the psychological aspects of denial, the emotional aspects of needing to perform, the professional pride of being reliable, and the financial necessity of not cancelling. I am particularly concerned when a singer travels and gets shots from doctors in different cities, just to get through the next show. That shot is usually just another form of cortisone, and the treatment shows a lack of foresight on the part of both physician and patient.

With regard to long and short-term effects of steroids, let me discuss a few items. Cortisone is often a good quick fix for inflammation, whether from an infection, allergy, or the trauma of excessive voice use. And there are definitely some performances that are potentially career making, which you simply need to get through. The problem comes when a singer relies on cortisone to get through most performances, neglecting the true nature of the problem (whether infection, allergy, or vocal trauma) and failing to address that.

In general, bacterial infections should not be treated with cortisone—it suppresses normal immune function which, through inflammation, helps your body to get rid of the infection. Viral infections, while not normally requiring specific antiviral medication, should be allowed to run their course, allowing the body's normal defences to get rid of the symptoms. And again, with allergies, the ideal treatment is to identify what you are allergic to and then either eliminate the allergens from your environment or get immunotherapy (injections) to reduce their effect. Finally, the treatment for vocal trauma is vocal rest and then a rethinking of what you are doing, either technically or by way of repertoire or performance schedule, that has made you hoarse. Treating the cause is always better than just ameliorating the symptoms.

Having said all of that, the short-term effects of cortisone can be beneficial at times for the voice. While some lower male voices experience a loss of high notes (a "ceiling effect") and some have also complained that the voice in general "sounds different," at least it's there, and you may get through your performance. This comes at the cost of increased appetite, elevated blood sugar, and a temporary suppression of immunity. Inhalants have less impact on the body, and act more locally. Steroid inhalers, usually used for asthma, can have a "quick-fix" effect if you are hoarse from vocal fold edema, if you are coughing from tracheitis, or are wheezing.

The long-term effect of steroids is more potentially hazardous. Repeated and regular steroid injections suppress your adrenal glands, leaving your defences weakened. It can cause diabetes, osteoporosis, and even necrosis of the femur (hip). It is associated with weight gain and skin changes. There are also psychological changes. Unfortunately, there are conditions (like severe arthritis or autoimmune diseases) that may require this treatment—but if you don't need it, why risk these things?

Steroid inhalers, while less systemically toxic, over time can cause yeast infection of the throat and larynx. It has been suggested that they can weaken the voice due to atrophy of the vocal muscles and weakening their contraction (steroid-induced myopathy). The result is a hoarseness that may be long term and this time will definitely not be cured by yet another cortisone injection.

What Are the Downsides of Anti-Depressants?

Dear Doctor Jahn,

I have recently been prescribed Prozac, 20 mg daily. Are there any possible effects on the larynx/singing voice that I should look out for, and, if so, what can I do to minimize them? - Olly

Dear Olly,

Prozac, an important and effective antidepressant, is widely used. I have many patients who take this medication, and none has reported a side effect specific to the voice. I do know that some antidepressants are drying, and you may need to increase your fluid intake. The PDR (Physician's Desk Reference) reports a small incidence of pulmonary problems, and if you develop difficulty breathing, you should certainly speak to your doctor and discontinue the medication. The mood-alteration of antidepressants and anti-anxiety medications are not specific in their effect on the voice, but certainly your vocal performance may be affected. To the best of my knowledge, none of these effects are permanent.

What is the Best Acne Treatment?

Dear Dr Jahn,

Which acne medications have the worst effect on the voice? I have been prescribed Accutane – what do you think of that? - Gina

Dear Gina,

Accutane is a Vitamin A analogue that is quite effective in cases of severe acne. I am assuming you have tried other acne medications, such as doxycycline and topical products, with no success. While these other medications have no adverse effect on the voice, unfortunately they are also not as effective for severe and potentially disfiguring acne. The main voice-related effect of Accutane is its drying effect on mucous membranes and skin. This is certainly reversible, and should disappear after you finish the medication, but you may have a dry larynx while taking the drug. Singing with a dry larynx makes it difficult to sing high notes softly, and you may find yourself muscling the notes more, increasing vocal effort to try to produce sounds that you could produce with less effort before. In turn, excess tension will affect your register change, creating a rough patch or even a yodel in the mix. Consider, also, that rubbing dry vocal folds together may predispose you to trauma at the vibrating edges, possibly leading to nodules.

As a solution, drink lots of water and consider taking a mucus thinner-type medication such as guaifenesin. There are various forms available; speak to your dermatologist or local laryngologist about this. Also, if you take vitamins, reduce or eliminate any Vitamin A while on Accutane, as the two are similar in some ways.

Will A Steroid Nasal Spray Make My Voice Raspy?

Dear Doctor Jahn,

I've been diagnosed with huge polyps in both nostrils and prescribed a cortisone nasal spray. I hesitate to take it because of its side effects, including throat raspiness. I earn a partial living singing and I'm anxiously awaiting your professional opinion. - Erin

Dear Erin,

If your polyps are truly "huge," meaning they obstruct your nasal passages completely or nearly completely, then it is unlikely that they will go away with a nasal spray, although they may decrease in size somewhat. My first suggestion is to find out why you have these. There are a number of conditions—such as allergies, aspirin sensitivity, and even chronic infections—that can cause polyps in the nose. Next, you need a CT scan to look at your sinuses and see how extensive the polyp formation is. Again, spraying the nose will not address the problem adequately if the polyps arise in the sinuses.

Once the underlying cause is discovered, it needs to be aggressively treated, including allergy management. If the polyps are truly extensive and obstructive, they should be removed rather than sprayed. This may also involve cleaning out your sinuses. As an alternative to removal, polyps may also be injected to reduce their size. But the most important thing is to address the underlying cause—if this is not treated, the polyps may recur despite adequate removal.

8. Master Reflux for Good

How Does Stomach Acid Reach the Voice?

Dear Doctor Jahn,

How does acid reflux actually irritate the voice? If acid is coming up in your esophagus, how does it irritate the vocal cords, given that they are in the wind pipe?
- Connie

Dear Connie,

Thank you for your thoughtful question. You're right, when stomach contents (acid and enzymes) reflux up the esophagus, they enter the throat behind the larynx.

Depending on the amount of material, it can spill over the ridge of tissue that separates the top of the esophagus from the larynx (the interarytenoid area), and cause irritation. In fact, this tissue between the arytenoid cartilages is often red and swollen with reflux, and this finding is one of the cardinal signs of acid reflux.

It is, however, extremely uncommon for acid to actually spill into the larynx or to damage the vocal folds directly. For this reason, I'm always upset when a doctor scares a singer by saying "your vocal cords are burned by acid". This is unnecessary fear mongering, and does the patient a disservice.

The commonest vocal effect of acid reflux is an irritation of the pharynx. This causes irritation of the muscles around the larynx and results in an elevation of the larynx. There are also neurologic receptors in the lining of the pharynx which, when irritated, cause the vocal folds to tighten and come together.

The net effect is an increase in muscle tension, which makes it more difficult to sing freely, causing problems negotiating the mix, and decreased resonance and power due to pharyngeal constriction.

What are the Side Effects to Reflux Medication?

Dear Doctor Jahn,

I've had years of reflux issues and I've been on PPIs (Proton Pump Inhibitor, a class of drugs that reduces acid secretion by the stomach cells) for years. Still my throat is feeling dry and raw, brittle, burning a little bit, trouble with high notes and stamina. I've tried going off PPI: some relief at first but then the symptoms return. Help! - Caroline

Dear Caroline,

A problem such as yours (really, any significant clinical problem) really requires a personal consultation and examination. Having said that, I do have a few suggestions for you to consider. First, are you overweight? You need to be at (or just below) your "ideal weight," for your height. So if that is an issue, I would recommend going on a diet to see whether this improves your symptoms.

While your observation that things improved when you went back on a proton pump inhibitor would suggest that you may indeed be refluxing, I would suggest a 24-hour pH probe study to document nocturnal (and daytime) reflux—the number of episodes and also the level to which the acid rises (this is done with a double probe). If this test is positive, it amounts to a "smoking gun" indicator that acid reflux is indeed your problem.

By way of treatment, and in addition to modifying what, when, and how much you eat (and drink), I would add Gaviscon liquid, which not only neutralizes acid but blocks it from coming up the esophagus. Also look at DGL, a form of liquorice which is helpful for acid reflux, is non-addictive, and has no side effects. You can buy this online.

Is it Possible to be Addicted to Reflux Treatment?

Dear Doctor Jahn,

I would really like to know if you encounter many singers who find themselves "dependent" on PPI drugs—that is, unable to find alternative treatments after having been on them long term? And if so, does this concern you from a medical perspective? - Dawn

Dear Dawn,

In answer to your question, please consider that PPIs have only been around for a few years, so no one really knows what a lifetime of medications would result in. Two significant concerns are increased osteoporosis and achlorhydria, decreased stomach acid. Osteoporosis, normally seen in post-menopausal women, occurs more frequently in men who take PPIs. The decrease in gastric acid can have consequences on vitamin B12 absorption. Neither of these issues is specific to singers, and I'm not sure they would have adverse effects specific to singing.

That said, I would suggest that before you commit to a lifetime on any medication, you exhaustively explore every other method of controlling your reflux, including dietary (what, when, and how much you eat), weight control, and alternative methods of controlling hyperacidity and reflux including herbal and homeopathic remedies, acupuncture, antacids, and an alkaline diet.

Are Antibiotics Giving Me Reflux?

Dear Doctor Jahn,

Is it possible to experience acid reflux after a course of antibiotics? - Jodie

Dear Jodie,

I read your e-mail with great interest. I don't have a simple answer for you. Clearly the antibiotics affect your stomach in a negative way which, interestingly, persists for some time. While an antibiotic may irritate the stomach during treatment, I am personally not aware that antibiotics trigger prolonged episodes of gastroesophageal reflux after treatment is over.

However, it is known that some antibiotics, such as Augmentin, can cause gastritis. Since the symptoms of gastritis overlap to some degree with the symptoms of GERD, I wonder whether this was the condition you actually developed. The symptoms of gastritis include epigastric pain and may create a sensation of burning and abdominal discomfort that can be confused with GERD. You should also be aware that during pregnancy and even afterward, patients may be more prone to reflux due to abdominal distention and a residual stretching of the hiatus in the diaphragm through which the esophagus passes.

I would also wonder whether you might have an H. pylori infection of the stomach, although I would expect such a bacterial infection to improve with antibiotics rather than get worse.

By way of treatment, you have not had good luck with the usual acid blockers. You may wish to consider DGL, a form of liquorice from which the blood pressure-raising component has been removed. This is a good natural way of controlling hyperacidity. You can purchase it online. I am also a fan of Gaviscon liquid, which not only neutralizes excess acid but also contains agar gel, which forms a mechanical barrier at the gastroesophageal junction, physically preventing the reflux of gastric contents up into the esophagus.

Your lump sensation (globus) is most likely the result of irritation of the upper end of the esophagus from reflux. If the reflux is effectively controlled and the sensation persists, you should consider acupuncture. I have treated a number of such patients with auricular acupuncture, and have had good results.

Can You Help My Problem with Swallowing?

Doctor Jahn,

My question pertains to a problem with swallowing. A couple of weeks ago, I almost choked on a piece of food and it seems that since then I have been overly conscious of swallowing. I am only able to swallow small pieces of food without making myself choke. Water is no problem, which tells me that there is nothing physically wrong with me. Do you have any idea how I might get back to swallowing normally? Any advice would be greatly appreciated. - Lily

Dear Lily,

This is an interesting problem. As you may know, swallowing has a conscious and a reflexive component. The oral phase (pushing the food to the back of the throat with the tongue) is conscious. Once the bolus of food gets past the back of the tongue, the reflexive, pharyngeal, part of swallowing occurs as a series of coordinated contractions which propel the food to the hypopharynx, and then through the esophagus to the stomach.

I would first make sure that you don't have acid reflux, which can irritate the sphincter at the upper end of the esophagus and make it too tight. Then, check that there is nothing anatomically wrong with your swallowing mechanism. There can be situations, such as a partial obstruction or muscle spasm, where liquids go down okay but solids don't. To evaluate this, you MAY need to get a cine barium swallow, which evaluates your swallowing process. If all of this is clear, I would see a swallowing therapist—this is a subspecialty of speech therapy that teaches patients (more often after a stroke or neurological problem) how to swallow. Of course, all of this should be directed and coordinated by a doctor, preferably a gastroenterologist.

Can Coffee Cause Reflux?

Dear Doctor Jahn,

I read your awesome answer on caffeine and the voice – but what about the effect of coffee on acid reflux? I've read that that is what's detrimental to the voice. What's your view? Also, what about pesticides on coffee beans – will that do me in? - Bill

Dear Bill,

In general terms, coffee, along with certain foods such as tomatoes, garlic, mint and grapefruit, can definitely cause acid reflux. In the case of coffee, it is probably not because of excess stomach acidity, but rather it may be due to a relaxation of the muscular valve (gastroesophageal sphincter) that separates the stomach and the esophagus.

But consider that caffeinated drinks, along with the "bad" foods, are something that most of us consume daily with no side effect, and certainly no effect on the voice. Further, many singers have some degree of reflux with no vocal impact. So some other things need to occur before coffee causes hoarseness.

If you are generally predisposed to reflux, because of obesity or because of your gastroesophageal anatomy, then yes, you should be careful. If you are slim and structurally "normal" but you drink 5 cups of coffee a day, along with your Coke, Red Bull, or other energy drinks, you may get reflux regardless of how competent your stomach and esophagus may be.

So, as always: all things in moderation. Incidentally, the most common effect of reflux on the throat is increased tension in the pharynx with elevation of the larynx. The vocal effects are most apparent in the mix (register shift) which becomes difficult to negotiate and cover.

Regarding the second question, I have no specific information on the voice effects of chemicals used in coffee processing, but reason dictates that coffee that has not been processed to remove caffeine (or processed using a water-based method) may be generally healthier.

Are My Wisdom Teeth Causing Vocal Trouble?

Dear Doctor Jahn,

I want to get rid of acid reflux. In my case I am wondering if it is possible that wisdom teeth on only the bottom jaw can cause throat problems and reflux? I only have wisdom teeth on the bottom jaw and I've had problems with my throat closing when I sing solo and acid reflux ever since they started coming in. - Jeremiah

Dear Jeremiah,

The short answer is: acid reflux cannot be caused by erupting wisdom teeth. But let's explore your symptoms.

How was your acid reflux diagnosed? I ask, because reflux to the back of the throat (called LPR, or laryngopharyngeal reflux) shares its symptoms with other conditions. These symptoms are rather nondescript, and include discomfort, cough, throat clearing and excess mucus and even earache.

My point is this: you may have symptoms such as pain in the throat or the ear from causes other than reflux, a diagnosis which is commonly - and not always accurately - made.
An erupting molar can cause earache by pain referred along shared nerves; it can also cause you to change your pattern of chewing and result in strain on the jaw joint (TMJ).
Local irritation can also cause pain in the adjacent base of tongue and throat.

Any irritation or muscle spasm in the area can cause an increase of muscle tone in the vocal tract, with an elevated larynx. This, in turn, can affect the voice, most specifically in the mix. So, if your vocal problems are in the mix (rather than the top), it may indirectly result from that erupting molar.

I suggest you take some antacid medications, both acid neutralizers and H1 blockers, to see if your voice improves. If not, I would question the original diagnosis of reflux.

Then, try some analgesics - perhaps apply a topical anesthetic to the tooth area, or take a mild muscle relaxant to address the theory of muscle tension secondary to pain and irritation. If this works, then you have your answer.

Does Reflux Make my Throat Tight?

Dear Dr. Jahn,

I have heard acid reflux can lead to throat tension. Is this true? How so? - Kate

Dear Kate,

This is my clinical observation: reflux is often associated with an elevated larynx, which is due to increased muscle tone. My explanation for the connection is this: when the mucosa of the pharynx is inflamed by reflux, it irritates the underlying muscles.

If the tone of the muscles attached to the pharynx and larynx is increased, the net effect is that the larynx moves up (there are many more elevators of the larynx than depressors). I think it is a reflex irritation, not a direct effect of the gastric juice on the muscles themselves. The problem is, of course, once you learn to phonate with higher muscle tension (whatever the cause), this may become your norm, and even if the reflux is completely controlled, you need to actively unlearn this method of phonation.

Can Reflux Cause Oral Yeast Infections?

Dear Doctor Jahn,

I have read a lot about low grade yeast infections. Does this affect the throat and the voice? I have not been on any antibiotics within the last two years and have never taken a steroid. Do you think that reflux could change the pH of the larynx such that yeast might be a problem for me? - Eddie

Dear Eddie,

While we do see low-grade yeast infections of the throat, this is a difficult area. In the absence of clear-cut signs of yeast, such as white patches in the pharynx and larynx, the diagnosis is more based on clinical suspicion than obvious clinical signs. As you are aware, many non-MD practitioners are proponents of systemic yeast infections being responsible for any number of symptoms. Their treatment includes blood tests, detoxifying diets, and therapy. I don't know enough about this to be either positive or negative, but the "yeast connection" is out there.

You mentioned some of the common factors that predispose to yeast infection: long term use of antibiotics or steroids. Others include asthma inhalers, diabetes and a suppressed immune system. In the absence of these, it would be unusual for you to develop a yeast infection, at least as most physicians understand it; your naturopath may disagree.

Regarding testing for yeast, my suggestion would be simpler—a short course of antifungal therapy to clean out whatever yeast might be there, and see whether your symptoms improve.

Are Antihistamines and Reflux Linked?

Dear Doctor Jahn,

I am writing about the supposed link between sinusitis and GERD [gastroesophageal reflux disease]. I have always had extremely bad seasonal allergies, and I have subjected myself to nose sprays, antihistamines, acupuncture, allergy shots, diet changes, nasal rinses - and I only see improvement with the latter. Western medicines are entirely too drying for me.

In relation to GERD, I began to experience the constant irritation and belching right around the time that the sinusitis took hold. I am very confident that in my body these are closely linked. I have gone to ENTs and had CAT scans, but no one has ever mentioned surgery. I know that my frontal and maxillary sinuses are clear, but my sphenoid

and ethmoid sinuses have blockage. It is accompanied by a constant postnasal drip, which has never been alleviated by any sprays and is the cause of irritation and throat tightness. Is surgery even an option with those cavities? - Faye

Dear Faye,

To answer your question first, GERD has now been implicated in sinusitis, because it seems that in some cases the reflux can actually travel up to the nasopharynx at night, causing an irritation and blockage of the sinuses. This is uncommon, but may occur.

In your case, this might be one possible explanation for your symptoms. You can put this to the test by taking an antacid at night, and sleeping somewhat elevated in bed, to see whether your symptoms improve. You may need to do this for a couple of weeks to see any results.

A second scenario would be that a chronic postnasal drip is creating irritation in the back of your throat, causing you to swallow frequently. Frequent "dry" swallowing (usually of air) is a common cause for belching. If you have significant sphenoid or ethmoid sinusitis, you should also normally also experience some headache or facial pain. If you don't have such pain, the CAT findings may not be relevant. You should, however, obtain a consultation with an ENT doctor.

Yes, these sinuses can be cleaned out, but if you were my patient, I would like to have a convincing clinical reason for doing so. Specifically, I would like to know whether the sinus changes on CT are cause or effect?

9. Women's Corner

Does Menstruation Make Me Sing Badly?

Dear Doctor Jahn,

A friend told me I should never sing in my pre-menstrual period. Is that good advice? Or, should I just ignore it?!
- Jen

Dear Jen,

"Never" is pretty harsh – it means that you are out of commission 25% of your career!

The real answer really depends on many things. First, what kind of singing do you do?

If you have a high soprano voice, the week before your period may certainly present some difficulties in singing high notes, especially soft and high singing.

Do you notice significant vocal changes during that week? Some women lose the ability to access their higher notes, and the sound does not project as well during this time. This is due to fluid retention not only in the vocal folds, but also the walls of the pharynx, which acts as an amplifier and resonator for the voice.

If you have significant PMS, singing during this time may require you to modify your technique - pushing and squeezing more - which not only produces a suboptimal voice, but needs to be undone once you are back to your post-period norm. With your doctor's advice, you may want to consider taking a mild diuretic to reduce fluid retention the week before your period.

Interestingly, all of these problems resolve once the period starts.

If you are among the fortunate minority who sail through their monthly cycle with no vocal problems, happy sailing! If, however, you do have significant difficulties before your periods, one option is to either cut back or change your performance schedule and repertoire to accommodate the limitation imposed by a sluggish and edematous (fluid retaining) vocal apparatus.

Another choice is to consider a form of long-term hormonal contraceptive therapy where you menstruate only 2-3 times a year. This limits the hormonal fluctuation and keeps your voice even and more predictable.

Best Way to Deal with Gynaecological Issues?

Dear Dr. Jahn,

I am a 48-year-old soprano with a flourishing career. I have uterine fibroids, which my gynecologist has been monitoring for about four years, and which have increased and grown to the point where my uterus is about twenty-week gestation size. My symptoms are currently primarily limited to the discomfort of the uterus being so large. My question to you has to do with evaluating the alternatives currently available to me for eliminating the fibroids in light of how each might affect my vocal apparatus and the systems involved in a singer's breathing capabilities.

I think I basically have three alternatives:

1) Have an abdominal hysterectomy for removal of the

uterus and fibroids.

2) Try to shrink the fibroids with Lupron therapy for a couple of months prior to a laparoscopic assisted vaginal hysterectomy of the uterus and fibroids.

3) Wait for menopause to shrink the fibroids. (I'm not real wild about this idea!)

I realize that you are not a gynecologist, but I would appreciate any suggestions. - Kim

Dear Kim,

First of all, you're right—I'm not a gynecologist. From the vocal point of view, however, I would be least excited about hormonal shrinking of the fibroids—if you're going to have a hysterectomy anyhow, what is the point? You may wish to consider a partial hysterectomy to allow the possibility of a future pregnancy. If not, then the hormone option is even less appropriate from a vocal point of view.

A couple of other thoughts regarding the voice. Consider that if you do have a hysterectomy, the effect from the vocal point of view of removing an enlarged uterus is similar to having suddenly lost weight. You will have to exercise afterwards (once healing is complete) to re-tighten the abdominal muscles and readjust your support.   Finally, if an abdominal incision is necessary, remind the surgeon that you do need those muscles to support the voice.

When is a Woman's Voice Finished Growing?

Dear Doctor Jahn,

How long will a young woman's voice continue to grow? What are the factors affecting how big a voice will get? My daughter is just a few months shy of 15. She has a fairly large and well developed voice for a 15-year-old. But we have been told that because of her petite, slender 5' 1" frame that her voice will probably not get large enough to be very competitive in the classical genres after the age of 18. - Ivy

Dear Ivy,

A number of factors can affect how long a young woman's voice continues to grow, some developmental and some technical. Developmentally, the voice will continue to grow for some time after menarche, and the best rough guide to whether she is "fully grown" would likely be bone age, which can be checked with a simple X-ray to look at the epiphyses (the ends of the hones). Of course, a fully grown young woman can he petite and slim, or tall, or more robust in size: the best indicator would be to look at the parents. Typically, teenagers grow in their trunk and extremities first, and the head assumes its adult dimensions last. Since the size and resonance of the voice relates not only to the size of the thorax (trunk) but also to the length of the vocal folds and the size of the resonating cavities above them, full growth can take several years. Now, the technical side. While the voice may be fully developed in terms of sheer power (i.e., lungs and vocal folds), it can continue to change in color and even register for many years during a singer's development. It is, for example, not unusual for mezzos to start with lighter roles such as Cherubino and then, over time, move to the heavier mezzo roles. The lighter soprano voices (like the souhrettes), in my opinion, do reach their full adult voice earlier than the more complex or dramatic ones. Like wine, voices can be fresh and fully developed early, or can take many years to mature and unfold. I hope this helps to answer your question.

Do Thyroid Medications Affect Singing?

Dear Doctor Jahn,

I read with interest your recent article on thyroid problems in women and singers. However, you leave out the next step: what will thyroid medication do for or against the voice? Is this a noticeable problem? The local nurses say it should make no difference and it may be they're right. On the other hand, they're awfully good at reassuring people. - Michelle

Dear Michelle,

The answer to your question is actually simple. If you are hypothyroid, which means "underactive," you should be on enough thyroid replacement medication to bring your levels up to normal thyroid, or "euthyroid," levels. If you overdose, the result is the same as having an overactive thyroid. The most noticeable effect on the voice would be a fine tremor. You would also have a number of non-vocal symptoms.

Will Hormones Cause Permanent Damage to my Voice?

Dear Doctor Jahn,

I am a high soprano and am considering donating my eggs for an infertile family. I really want to do it, but I wonder what the hormone injections will do to my voice. Would there be irreversible damage to the cords or a temporary change in the voice? Anything else I need to consider besides the general risks? - Georgia

Dear Georgia,

The short answer to your question is: I don't know. The longer answer is: it depends on what the injections consist of. If it is estrogen, there should be no problem. If it is gonadotropin, I would also think no problem. Also, it would be for a short period of time (i.e. until you ovulate), so any changes should be reversible. Since this is an elective procedure, however (and I applaud the generosity of your gesture), you should check things out with the gynecologist and online.

Can I Find My Pre-Pregnancy Voice?

Dear Doctor Jahn,

Since giving birth (6 times!), and at age 40, I am finally returning to singing. I'm concerned that I no longer seem to have the range and vocal capacity I had in my 20s. Will my voice ever return to its former state? - Andrea

Dear Andrea,

First, let me congratulate you for ensuring that the next generation of singers will be there for all of us to enjoy! Your question has so many ramifications that I can only point you in some general directions to think about.

First, have you been singing all along, or are you now returning after a prolonged absence? If the second, consider that you need to gradually work into your voice, a sort of accelerated "learn to sing" program. Make sure all the mechanics are in place: low larynx, open throat, low tongue, connecting the breath to the voice - all the principles you hopefully learned when you sang earlier.

Then, take a sober look at your instrument, including pelvis and abdomen as well as thorax and vocal tract. If you have gained weight and lost abdominal muscle tone, this will affect your support and your stamina. If you compensate for this by muscling the larynx and pharynx, that will also change your tone and possibly your range. So, if necessary, lose weight and tone up.

Regarding your range, there is no reason why, at 40, your range should have changed. Consider, however, that at any time in a singer's career, the voice may change, unrelated to past pregnancies, deliveries or hormones. You need to re-explore your voice almost as a new instrument. You may find that the voice has darkened - perhaps you gained some notes on the bottom, and the top is less clear than it was. Before throwing in the towel, start working with a good teacher to see what you really have. You may just be out of practice. As a colleague once observed, many a "mezzo" is just a lazy soprano.

Finally, as you start to sing, begin well within your comfort zone and work outward. Don't try to sing things that were an effort even twenty years ago, but work towards that. Be focussed in the moment, but also kind to yourself.

Will the Pill Deepen my Voice?

Dear Doctor Jahn,

I've heard anecdotal evidence from singer friends about birth control pills affecting the voice in terms of some loss of range and flexibility. Is there scientific evidence that backs this up? What is the safest form of birth control for a singer? - Sally

Dear Sally,

A couple of years ago we ran a survey canvassing singers about their own experiences. In brief, we believe that BC pills that contain synthetic progestins may darken some voices, particularly the higher and lighter soprano voices. This is because synthetic progestins metabolize into a testosterone analog (androgenic), which can masculinize the voice.

How individuals react to specific oral contraceptives is unfortunately idiosyncratic and somewhat unpredictable. If you have a high and light soprano voice and plan to take BC pills for birth control (rather than to regulate your periods) you may want to look at alternative methods of contraception such as an IUD, preferably one that does not elute hormone.   In any case, discuss with your gynecologist what is in the BC pill that she/he plans to prescribe. I cannot refer you to a specific authoritative article on the topic, but am sharing with you what our current thinking is. I'm sure you will find relevant articles by the appropriate key words online.

Is Breastfeeding Tightening my Voice?

Dear Doctor Jahn,

I am a 27-year-old soprano and a new mom, breast feeding my 4-month old baby. My pregnancy and delivery were easy and uneventful. During my pregnancy I experienced perfect vocal health; I sang recitals and even sang a show. I am breastfeeding and since the delivery I have run into a number of problems. I know there is a breastfeeding hormone that can affect the top notes—make the cords tight and not easily stretched, which I am experiencing. But the bigger problem is something else. Directly in my middle

range, the B, C, C#, and D above middle C are rough, almost like radio static. I am wondering if you know anything about this and if I can blame the breastfeeding or the delivery on this problem? - Faith

Dear Faith,

I don't have a clear answer to your question, but I do have some thoughts. Problems in the middle range may be due to swelling on the vocal folds. However, if your top is clear, the problem is more likely one of muscular incoordination. By this I don't mean inadequate support, but more to do with the laryngeal muscle repositioning that is involved in the mix. My suggestion would be to undergo videostroboscopy with a good laryngologist to look for any incoordination in that range, and then you may need to work that part of the voice or even consider shifting your register change temporarily. Again, I am not a voice therapist, and these are just suggestions. The condition may improve significantly once you stop lactating.

Can I Regain my Pre-Birth Control Range?

Dear Doctor Jahn,

Will going off the Pill after several years straight affect my range – I am hoping it might increase it! - Debbie

Dear Debbie,

Hormones do affect the voice. Although most laryngologists agree that there are no specific estrogen receptors on the vocal folds, many singers have noticed that once they start oral contraceptives, they lose a little bit off the top. They may also gain a bit on the bottom, but usually less. This effect is probably related to the specific hormone preparation, but is also to some degree idiosyncratic. The important point for you, however, is that this effect is not reversible. Going off the Pill will not change your voice, and your range will remain the same whether you give the Pill "a rest" or continue. Unless your voice is still developing, your next possible voice change should not occur until the menopause. If you are comfortable with the oral contraceptive preparation you are taking, from the vocal point you should stay with it. If you change your Pill, there may be additional voice changes. In general, take the least amount of hormone you need to regulate your cycle.

Will Pregnancy Hormones Wreck My Voice?

Dear Doctor Jahn,

I may have to undergo some treatments if I want to get pregnant, including regular doses of progesterone and clomide, but I am afraid of the side effects on my voice. In general, what are your thoughts on this? - Gillyanne

Dear Gillyanne,

Infertility treatments involve injections that reset the hormonal cycle and can have significant effects on the voice. The vocal folds can become more vascular, and there is a higher incidence of hemorrhage. Most singers find a significant, although ill-defined, effect on the voice, and it might be wise to stop singing while the treatments are in effect. Long term effects are less predictable, and according to patients I have spoken with, there may in fact be no long-term adverse effect. In general, hormone treatments affect the higher, lighter voices more, so your voice type may also be a factor.

Will the Pill Bring Back my Low Notes?

Dear Dr Jahn,

Question: I am a 31-year-old soprano. I have discovered that in the days leading up to my menstruation and during it, the low and middle part of my voice do not phonate.

Colleagues have suggested going on the pill to manipulate my cycle so that I am not experiencing the above-mentioned problems, especially if I have a performance. I would appreciate any thoughts you may have on the subject and welcome any information and advice you can offer. Also, I take a small dose of Propranolol (5 mg) before a performance to help with nerves. To your knowledge, does this medication affect singing? - Jeanette

Dear Jeanette,

The middle- and low-voice difficulties you experience are likely not related to a swelling of the vocal folds themselves, but more to general fluid retention in the tissues of the pharynx, and even the muscles that move the vocal folds and raise and lower the larynx in the neck. I suspect this is the case: since you had swelling of the vocal folds only, your problem would be in high voice. You could try a mild diuretic about a week before your period; try the herbal ones first. Also, try to cut back your sodium (salt) intake. Be aware that during the premenstrual phase, many women actually crave salt.

The pill can regulate your cycle, but I'm not sure it would reduce your premenstrual vocal problems: it does help some women with premenstrual cramping and more systemic symptoms. The pill can, however, alter your voice a bit, and more significantly if you have a high voice.

Propranolol is often used for performance anxiety. Five milligrams isn't a high dose and shouldn't affect you adversely. Some feel it takes the "edge" off the performance, but if for you that "edge" equates with terror, it might be a worthwhile trade-off.

Is PMS Making my Voice Breathy?

Dear Doctor Jahn,

Could you address the effect of PMS on the voice? PMS tends to take away the "glow" from my sound; the cords don't come together as cleanly, and there is a veneer of air around the sound. Do you have any suggestions on how to help alleviate the problem? I know that exercise and certain vitamins such as the B complex help other PMS symptoms. I also know that some women find relief by taking birth-control pills. Can these methods also help the voice? - Sara

Dear Sara,

Let me preface this by saying that I am neither a gynecologist nor an endocrinologist. My understanding of premenstrual voice problems is that female hormones, progesterone in particular, lead to fluid retention. They also change the viscosity of the ground substance in the cells, causing a stiffening or thickening of the vocal folds. This typically makes the voice less flexible, more unwieldy, and takes some of the ring out of the voice.

Treatment? It depends on how much this encumbers your singing. In the same way that some women have minimal premenstrual problems versus others who suffer greatly, the voice can also be affected a little or a lot. If you retain a great deal of fluids, you may consider a mild diuretic in the week before your period. If periods are heavy, crampy and uncomfortable, oral contraceptives may help. There is also a wealth of alternative-medicine-type herbs and vitamins that may be of benefit.

I would suggest you consult a gynecologist or a naturopath. As a final point, the problems, both systemic and vocal, may be greater at the extremes of your reproductive span, i.e. shortly after the menarche and before menopause.

I'm Clueless About Hormone Replacement Therapy

Dear Dr. Jahn,

I was wondering if you could provide any advice on considerations and recommendations for hormone replacement therapy. I am planning to go on some kind of HRT, but I have no idea if there are any that are better for singers than others, etc. I feel that many women singers will be interested in this. Thanks for any advice or information to which you can direct me. - Annette

Dear Annette,

From the vocal point of view, HRT is definitely beneficial: it keeps the tissues moist, flexible and young. The real question pertains to other concerns with HRT, such as heart attacks and strokes. If there is no significant history of these conditions in your family, you are probably at low risk, and, after discussion with your gynecologist, may decide to take HRT after menopause.

As to what is best, this is not clear. Some advocate natural sources of estrogen such as soy, black cohosh, and other herbal sources. This sounds more holistic than synthetic hormones, but there have been no studies to show that the potential side effects are any less than with conventional hormone replacement. Either way, estrogen gets to your tissues, and is helpful for your voice. Avoid synthetic testosterone, since it can darken the voice—you would of course not normally take this. Do have a detailed discussion with your gynecologist.

10. Before and After Surgery

How Can I Recover from Nodules?

Dear Doctor Jahn,

It has been over 6 months since my nodules healed and I have had several successful performances where my voice is behaving reasonably well, but there are many times where I seem to be going backwards. The littlest things seem to throw my voice into a tailspin for days and days! Also, my very highest notes have still not come back since my vocal injury. Any advice? - Kathy

Dear Kathy,

I have a number of questions for you, which should be considered. Did the nodules resolve spontaneously, or did you have surgery? If spontaneously resolved, did this happen solely because of voice rest, or due to voice therapy or a change in repertoire and technique? If the nodules were surgically removed, was this done with a laser, or microsurgery?

In general, nodules are not a disease, but a sign of excessive or inappropriate voice use.

To completely treat the nodules, it is essential that you change how you use your voice, both in performance and socially. Often, a singer can modify their vocal technique, but continues to abuse the speaking voice, either due to habit or because of the demands of a day job.

So, a complete evaluation and vocal overhaul is necessary, under the watchful guidance of an experienced voice therapist. I compare nodules to corns on your toes: they result from wearing ill-fitting shoes (or using an inappropriate voice). You can remove the corns surgically, but unless you also change your shoes, they will inevitably come back.

But let's assume that the nodules are truly gone, and you have changed your technique, your venue, and your repertoire.

Consider two other confounders: the first is the need to get rid of any pre-treatment compensatory behavior. This means that if you were singing adequately with your nodules, this usually requires excessively squeezing the vocal folds together, tightening the pharynx, raising the larynx and in general "muscling" the voice, rather than singing with good bottom-up support and a relaxed upper vocal tract.

You may have hung on to this compensatory behavior after your treatment, but now the compensation which was a necessary evil before has no place, and has, in turn, become the disease. So, both nodules and faulty vocal technique need to be changed.

The second issue, of course, is any scarring from your surgery. This can happen with laser treatment as well as conventional removal. If the vocal folds are left stiff, it becomes difficult to sing softly at the top of your range. You may, in particular, note difficulties around F5 (top line of the staff) and up.

By pushing in this range, you may again revert to "muscling", and the vicious cycle starts again.

Two suggestions – one, consider that scars (no matter how microscopic) take about six months to completely heal, at the end of which time they are as small and as soft as they will be. So continue to work the voice, especially with exercises like a "siren" or glissando, which stretch the vocal folds. Hydrate assiduously.

If the problem remains, consider having a stroboscopic examination to check for stiffness.

It is best to do this with a laryngologist, who may be in a position to offer you treatment.

Treatment options include injection of cortisone and elevation of the scarred area by injection of saline, as well as aggressive voice therapy.

Is it Nodules or a Polyp?

Dear Dr Jahn,

I'm confused. I have developed a hoarse voice, and saw a couple of ENT doctors. One said I had a nodule, the other one thought I had a polyp. Are they not the same thing?
- Cora

Dear Cora,

In fact, polyps and nodules of the vocal folds are quite different entities, both in how they develop, and how they should be treated.

Vocal fold nodules are like calluses that form when the vocal folds are habitually rubbed together with excessive force. They are classically seen on both vocal folds, and form at the point of maximal trauma, one third of the way back from the front of the larynx. They are generally symmetrical, and may be small or large, soft or firm.

The treatment for nodules is to change how you use your voice: less force, less "muscling", more support and a mixed belt. Simple removal, whether with instruments or a laser, usually doesn't solve the problem, since continued vocal abuse will simply cause them to recur.

So, therapy. is the answer. Rarely, surgery will help to make therapy more effective, but do not run to have them removed without working on your technique.

Polyps, by contrast, are usually only on one vocal fold; these develop after a hemorrhage.
While most hemorrhages will resolve completely with strict voice rest, if you are not aware that you have had some bleeding into the vocal fold and continue to sing, you may well form a polyp.

Polyps are not a sign of poor technique. They simply form when there has been an episode (usually a single episode) of vocal trauma resulting in bleeding. They do not indicate chronic vocal abuse. So, unlike for nodules, the treatment for polyps involves medication (cortisone), and then possibly surgical removal – ideally by a surgeon who treats singers.

I would advise someone like you to get a third (deciding) opinion. As you see, polyps and nodules are quite different, and require different management for a good result.

What Vocal Rest Do I need After Laryngeal Surgery?

Dear Doctor Jahn,

I have some kind of sore or lesion on my false folds (I'm told it is not cancer) and am having surgery so that the doctors can get a "piece" of it to examine further – since it just doesn't go away. I have some gigs coming up and want to know what kind of voice rest (total?) I need after this surgery before I can sing – when can I start rehearsing after

this operation? One week? Then, when can I expect my voice be back to normal? I stress that we are talking about the false folds rather than the vocal folds themselves. - Diane

Dear Diane,

If we're talking about a small biopsy, there are three main post-op issues.

I am making the assumption that this is a small benign lesion, that the procedure is done carefully, without excessive tissue removal or bleeding, and your anesthesiologist is also skilful. The issues pertain to postoperative discomfort, swelling, and the irritation to the true vocal folds from intubation.

Some discomfort is possible, and this may be felt in the throat as well as the ear on the same side. This in turn may cause some splinting, i.e. elevation of the larynx, when you sing, causing you to muscle the voice.

The amount of actual swelling at the biopsied site may vary. If significant, it can temporarily reduce vocal projection, since the "ring" in the voice (the singer's formant) is generated in the ventricle, the hollow area between the true and false fold. Finally, you may have some true vocal fold swelling from being intubated.

To specifically answer your questions, I would put you on modified voice rest (no singing or loud speaking, talk minimally in a "confidential voice" only) for one week. The second week, start vocalizing, and after two full weeks, you can start performing.

Just one more thought – some laryngologists are able to do the biopsy in their office under local anaesthetic, without the need to be put to sleep and intubated. Something to consider.

Will a Nose Job Change my Voice?

Dear Doctor Jahn,

Thank you so much for this opportunity to ask you questions about medical problems and their relation to our voice! My question is about rhinoplasty. When I was 11 years old, I broke my nose in an accident. It is now bent to one side and has a large bump that can be seen when looking at my profile. I'm still able to breathe but only through one nostril. I am now 20 years old and have thought about getting it fixed. I'm just really worried that it might affect my resonance or breathing or change my voice somehow. - Jenn

Dear Jenn,

From your description, it does sound like you would benefit from surgery, both to correct your deviated septum and possibly to improve the cosmetic appearance. It has been my experience, after performing many procedures on singers, that the voice does change after nasal surgery. This change, however, is usually for the better! Particularly in patients with nasal obstruction, they find that their post-operative voice is bigger and more forward. They are now able to gain more resonance in the mask with less effort. This is due to increased space in the nasal cavities. I have even had patients tell me that they can now access notes that they couldn't reach before. I find this more difficult to explain than the mask issue, but am relating to you what patients have told me.

I have two concerns regarding your surgery. One, please make sure that your doctor doesn't reduce the overall size of your nose excessively—this could have a negative effect, especially if you develop scarring from the incisions inside the nostrils. The other important issue: please make sure the septal deviation is fully corrected. From the vocal point of view, appearance is less of a concern than function.

Should I have my Snoring Tonsils Removed?

Dear Doctor Jahn,

I have a history of snoring and some sleep apnea. I went to the ENT a while back to get something checked out in my throat, and he told me that my tonsils were larger than they should normally be and it may be the cause of my snoring. He advised I have them removed to see if that helps with the apnea. As a singer, I would like to know the risks associated with having this surgery performed, and if the benefits outweigh them. - Craig

Dear Craig,

Certainly, massive tonsils can obstruct the oropharynx, and it can fall back into the throat at night (especially if you sleep on your back), causing snoring and exacerbating a possible sleep apnea. You could test this hypothesis by trying to sleep with the head of the bed elevated, and sleeping on your side. I have had a number of patients with large tonsils who have no obstruction, although some of them have learned to sleep on their belly, presumably to keep the tonsils away from the back of the throat.

One thing is certain: as a generally healthy adult, you have no need for your tonsils. In general, a tonsillectomy, properly done, should have no adverse effect on the voice. Some singers actually feel there is more room in the back and find that the voice comes more forward and sounds less covered once large tonsils are removed.

I'm Scared to Have Sleep Apnea Surgery!

Dear Doctor Jahn,

My ENT has suggested that he perform a UPPP [Uvulopalatopharyngoplasty] on me in order to treat sleep apnea. (He uses the new technique using ultrasound). I'm a serious amateur singer, and am a bit concerned about what effect this procedure might have on my voice. My ENT showed me, in a mirror, that my throat opening is quite small (and I have an unusually large uvula). Can you comment as to whether a UPPP would help, hurt, or be neutral with respect to my singing and speaking voice? Also, can you say how effective it might be in treating the sleep apnea? - Chris

Dear Chris,

A UPPP (or versions of it) reduces the length and flaccidity of the soft palate, and is often dramatically helpful in eliminating snoring. Sleep apnea can occur with snoring, but the two are not identical: some people snore loudly with no sleep apnea, while others have sleep apnea but do not snore.

Regarding the effect on your voice, there is always some worry that the palate may not work as well as it did before the procedure, although in most cases it isn't a problem. I have done this surgery on a few singers, and it turned out well, but I wouldn't normally jump to palate surgery in singers.

Have you discussed using a CPAP [Continuous Positive Airway Pressure] machine rather than surgery? It might be a good option. If you cannot use the CPAP machine, and there are really no other options (such as significant sleep apnea with severe oxygen desaturation), I would suggest that the procedure be

145

done conservatively (less tissue removal). I have had no personal experience with an ultrasound device for this condition.

Is it Wise to Remove Wisdom Teeth?

Dear Doctor Jahn,

I am preparing for graduate school auditions and scheduling the removal of my wisdom teeth. First, will having all four teeth removed have any effect on my vocal production? Secondly, the oral surgeon mentioned that after the surgery I am not supposed to put any excess pressure on my sinuses, such as blowing my nose too hard. For most people this would not be a problem, but does it mean that I will not be able to sing? If so, for how long? My teeth are not causing me pain now, but I don't have much room and would rather have them removed sooner than later. - Lizzy

Dear Lizzy,

Removal of the wisdom teeth is usually done electively (rather than as an emergency), so if your oral surgeon thinks this may be useful, I would go along with that. Just ask why he recommends this: for crowding, potential infection, etc.

There are a number of potential complications for singers with this type of surgery that you should know about, and discuss with your doctor. They include (1) injury to the lower jaw nerve, either from injection or from the extraction; (2) an abnormal opening into the maxillary sinus when the upper wisdom teeth are removed, and (3) prolonged TMJ dysfunction, either from the surgery or from keeping your mouth open during the procedure. The nerve injury, specifically, can leave you with prolonged or permanent numbness to the chin or lower lip. Of course, most of the time these things do not happen, but you need to be aware that any "routine" surgery can occasionally lead to difficulties.

How Do I Gain my Pre-Op Breathing Power?

Dear Doctor Jahn,

I've had an operation. Two months later and I get breathless on exertion and sometimes make involuntary gasps. What is the best way to build my breathing – just deep breathing and exercise? I want to get back to singing! The operation involved a ventilator which left some scarring and water on my lungs (laparotomy followed by an abdominal drain insertion due to sepsis.)
- Theresa

Dear Theresa,

Wow, you've had quite a serious problem! Hopefully you have fully recovered from your illness. The complete answer to your query would be very long, so let me just make some suggestions:

First, you need to make sure that all medical issues are out of the way. Is there any residual fluid or scarring in the lungs? I suggest that you first see a pulmonologist to make sure your lungs are fully functional – this might require a pulmonary function test.

Next, I would like to know whether your surgery was done laparoscopically or with an open abdominal incision? If there were any incisions thorough the abdominal muscles, that might affect your ability to contract them during exhalation and vocalization.

Next I wonder about what has happened inside your abdomen. Do you have any scarring, adhesions, or discomfort on deep breathing or pushing? Have you lost a significant amount of weight in the course of your illness?

All of these issues might affect your breathing and your vocal support. Once all of these possibilities have been addressed, you should consider deep breathing exercises, and possibly yoga breathing to refocus your breathing.

And then, it's time to work with a good voice therapist to address issues like reconnecting the breath to the voice and support.

Tonsil Scarring is Dampening my Voice

Dear Doctor Jahn,

I had my tonsils removed three years ago, in response to chronic tonsillitis. Fast forward to now: I have been working with a vocal coach, and a consistent problem seems to be lowering of the soft palate, especially as I sing descending scales, causing me to lose resonance and vibrato and even sag in pitch. I've noticed since the operation that there are small areas of scarring in the back of my throat where the incisions were made. Could these be inhibiting the free movement of the palate and causing these problems? What can I do to remedy this? Is additional treatment necessary to alleviate this if this is indeed the case? - Laura

Dear Laura,

When the tonsils are removed, they are separated from the two sides of the pharynx, leaving a raw area that heals over time. During the healing process there is, of course, swelling and some stiffness of the palate, but this healing should be complete, returning to normal within three months. Naturally, after any surgery there is some residual scar, but your question pertains to whether this scar is functionally significant.

In my experience, if the surgery is done carefully and without any unexpected complications such as excessive bleeding (which requires cauterization or suturing), there should be no difficulty lifting the palate. Keep in mind that every time you swallow you need to lift your palate to completely occlude the nasopharynx (i.e., the palate must close against the back of the pharynx), otherwise you would reflux your drink into your nose. So your palate obviously moves, and moves well. It is possible that your proprioception (your body's sense of position) in the area has changed, but this should not affect actual movement.

You may wish to consult a speech pathologist to assess how effectively you are able to lift the palate and to see whether both sides of the palate move equally well. She may even give you exercises to strengthen the palate—exercises that they use to treat patients who have true velopharyngeal incompetence. I would not have any further surgery done to loosen the palate. Keep in mind, also, that cortisone injections can cause the muscle to weaken or atrophy.

My Post-Op Voice Feels Strange

Dear Doctor Jahn,

I had my appendix removed Friday, Sept. 23. I am still recovering, but I noticed my voice does not seem the same. I do not have the same sensation when I am singing as well. Can you please explain why this is happening? - Miles

Dear Miles,

I received your question on Sept. 28, so I will assume you wrote it on the 27th. Your question is why does your voice not feel normal four days after a general anesthetic and an abdominal operation?

I am purposely restating your question to make a point: four or five days after this sort of surgery, it would be unusual if your voice were normal! And there are many possible reasons, including the intubation during anesthesia, some dehydration, and some of the medications you may have been given, which could be drying. A second group of possible causes have to do with difficulty supporting after an abdominal incision, and possible change in bowel habits. All of these are temporary. I would recommend patience, lots of fluids, and allowing your body to return to its normal state.

When should you start to sing? I suggest 7-10 days after your surgery. Although your appendectomy was probably done laparoscopically, which is a much smaller incision with less effect on your bowel habits, you still need to wait this long for swelling, dehydration, etc., to correct themselves. When you do start singing, work on getting your larynx back into normal singing position and focus on your abdominal support, which may be temporarily impaired. Don't push and don't be impatient. Give your body time to heal. Of course, if you continue to have problems that are not improving after two weeks, you should consult an ENT doctor for a look at your vocal tract.

Can Tonsils Cause Hoarseness?

Dear Doctor Jahn,

One of my voice students has been complaining of severe allergies all semester. She's been too hoarse to sing, and even when her voice got better and her speaking voice was mostly clear, after a few trial runs it became apparent to me that she shouldn't be singing right now. I sent her to an ENT who said her cords were okay and gave her the go-ahead to sing, but said that her tonsils need to come out and that's why her throat and neck are so sore. She says she is no longer hoarse (I haven't heard her - we've been e-mailing). Would you agree that her symptoms are the results of her tonsils, and would having them removed address her problems? - Denisa,

Dear Denisa,

The real question here is: are her tonsils responsible for her hoarseness? The usual story with chronic tonsillitis is that patients get recurrent sore throats, especially when their immune systems are run down. So if your student gets sore throats and then tries to sing using compensatory muscle positioning to get the voice out, leading to hoarseness, maybe having her tonsils out would be reasonable.

Is she hoarse when trying to sing with the sore throat? Or is the hoarseness unrelated to her sore throats? If hoarseness follows singing with a sore throat, and sore throats are a frequent occurrence, having the tonsils out may be a useful option. If the two are unrelated, a tonsillectomy might not help.

Can Tonsils Cause Trouble for the Voice?

Dear Doctor Jahn,

What effect do the tonsils—or the removal of the tonsils— have, if any, on the singing voice? I can feel my uvula when I sing, now that they are removed. - Dave

Dear Dave,

The tonsils play an important and active role in young children— they help to acquire immunity for the body. In adults, however, they are inactive, usually rudimentary, and have no function. When these small and scarred tonsils are removed (hopefully for a good reason), there is usually no effect on the voice. When the tonsils are huge, however, singers often tell me they feel they have more room in the back of the throat.

Large tonsils which are chronically infected can encumber palate movement to a minor degree. When enormous, they can create a hypo nasal, "hot potato" voice. Proper removal, in turn, can allow greater freedom and flexibility in the back of the throat. This removal must, however, preserve as much mucous membrane as possible, with minimal scarring of the base of the soft palate on either side. A surgeon who is familiar with the mechanics of singing should do it.

Can Wind Instruments Cause Nodules?

Dear Dr. Jahn,

I am a 19-year-old junior at college majoring in voice and bassoon. I recently went to a voice clinic to get my voice checked out because I was experiencing airiness and a voice teacher had suggested it. I found out that I had a vocal callus, and the otolaryngologist I went to was not sure what had caused the callus. He was not sure if it was my singing, speaking, or bassoon playing that had caused it. Do you have any suggestions? - Andi

Dear Andi,

I am not clear on the term "vocal callus." I assume your doctor is referring to a nodule? Nodules normally occur in pairs, one on each vocal fold, so if you only had one "callus," it might be something else, such as a bit of thickening which is the fibrous residuum of a vocal polyp. So the first thing is to figure out what he really saw, since the treatment for the two conditions is quite different.

Assuming you're well hydrated, airiness in the voice, especially on top, normally means that the vocal folds are not approximating. This can be the result of a mass on the vocal fold, such as a polyp, nodule, or "callus." It can also be the result of how you posture your vocal folds—using excess muscle tension prevents the vocal folds from properly approximating.

Regarding the bassoon: in my opinion, this is good for a singer. It teaches you to exhale against resistance, to manage your breath, and to open the upper airway. There is, of course, some tension in the mouth itself as you hold the double reed, but I think most would agree that any wind instrument, especially a double reed, is not harmful for singers.

Will a Tummy Tuck Decrease my Vocal Power?

Dear Doctor Jahn,

I have lost about 75 pounds and have excess skin in my abdominal area. It is bothersome because it really distorts my figure and I have to constantly wear a girdle. I am considering having a tummy tuck but am concerned about how the surgery would affect my voice since the abdominal muscles are "tightened" during surgery. Another option would be a panniculotomy, which only removes the skin. Do you know how these surgeries might affect the voice? I have searched everywhere for this information but can't find anything. Any information or help you can give me would be great. - Joanne

Dear Joanne,

To get the full answer to your questions (and certainly if you are considering this surgery), you really need to talk to a surgeon who specializes in this kind of procedure, either a bariatric surgeon or a plastic surgeon. My experience with singers who have lost a lot of abdominal weight, either from surgery or drastic dieting, is that they have difficulty supporting the voice. They really have to rework the breath until the abdominal muscles have adjusted to their new "resting position." Removal of just abdominal skin and fat (superficial to the muscles) should not have any effect on your voice. Suturing the muscles (primarily the rectus abdominis muscles in the front) might alter their range of contraction, but I suspect with adequate work you should be able to retrain these muscles to adequately support the voice.

11. Dealing with Asthma and Allergies

Can Asthma Treatment Ruin my Singing?

Dear Doctor Jahn,

I've been having trouble with my voice lately. When I put weight onto it, I become hoarse and end up marking (not singing out in full voice). This is a problem now, since I'm in rehearsals. Having allergies and asthma, I have been taking Advair once a day. Have you heard of any problems with that steroid spray? My general practitioner mentioned the other day that Advair does affect the voice. - Yvette

Dear Yvette,

I would consider two possible causes. First, Advair does indeed cause hoarseness, and should not be used unless there is no alternative for asthma. This medication is often prescribed because it combines two different medications for asthma - a steroid and a bronchodilator. You can replace this with other combination formulations which may also work for you.

Second, with any steroid inhaler there is a possibility of yeast infection. You should be checked for this, and given antifungal medications if necessary. An early yeast infection can at times cause only dryness and redness, without the classic white patches, so it is easy to miss.

Asthma Symptoms Are Holding Me Back

Dear Doctor Jahn,

I am a low-voiced male with a larger voice. I am actually singing pretty well and am lucky enough to be working in some major venues, but I could still use some help to reach my full potential. I have both allergies and asthma, and I feel that my stamina and range could improve if my throat wasn't always so irritated. An hour per day of singing is plenty for me. And that's not really enough for the rehearsal process. I also wake up with about an added fifth on the bottom of my range. This thickness is fun to play with but bad for those early rehearsals! I've tried Singulair; it's helped but has caused reflux. - Gary

Dear Gary,

Let's talk about those allergies. What are you allergic to? Can you minimize your allergy and asthma symptoms by identifying and reducing/eliminating these substances from your environment? A good allergy consultant can help you with this, and might even recommend desensitization shots. While tedious, these eliminate the usually drug-related side effects that allergy sufferers complain of.

Singulair is a good drug, and if it controls your symptoms, might be a good one to continue. There are newer studies that recommend 10 mg twice a day rather than once a day, and my allergist colleagues tell me that the effect can be significantly enhanced. If you are convinced that Singulair exacerbates your reflux, you could consider a simple oral antacid such as Gaviscon, rather than starting on the more expensive anti-GERD meds like Nexium. Consider also taking the Singulair in the morning, when you have a full vertical day ahead, rather than a horizontal night.

Other treatments for allergies include herbal medications such as stinging nettle capsules. A consultation with a Traditional Chinese Medicine (TCM) practitioner who is versed in herbal medication would be a different but potentially good avenue for you.

Regarding your asthma, you again need to diagnose whether it is allergic or not (other forms include exercise or cold-induced asthma, or infectious asthma). Acupuncture can be very useful for some cases and, again, has the benefit of no side effects. You could explore this with a good acupuncturist.

Would an Asthma Inhaler Make the Voice Feel Sluggish?

Dear Doctor Jahn,

I am a physician with a singer patient who has moderate asthma and requires inhaled cortisone. She notes her vocal cords feel heavy and less flexible. She is a high soprano and reports that her vibrato is slow. What suggestions do you have for her? I appreciate your comments. - William

Dear William,

I'm assuming that you can't control her asthma with oral medications or non-steroidal inhalers. I'm also assuming that this is intrinsic asthma, and not one where allergic or other triggers can be identified and eliminated.

I would use QVAR rather than Advair, and add a separate bronchodilator if necessary. You could also consider other combination steroid/bronchodilator preparations such as Symbicort. I would also use a steroid (if possible) that does not have any powder or chemical propellant, and I would ask her to use the inhaler only when absolutely necessary. I would also explore acupuncture treatments, which can be highly effective for some cases of asthma.

If she absolutely cannot avoid inhaled steroids, and you are convinced that this is the cause of her hoarseness, make sure she is well hydrated (8-10 glasses of water a day). She may also need to rework her technique using a bit more laryngeal pressure (vs. an open larynx and supporting the voice from below only). This kind of voice is often acceptable for musical theatre or popular music.

Finally, please consider the possibility of an acquired yeast infestation of the larynx, which can worsen hoarseness, along with other symptoms such as discomfort on swallowing.

Is my Asthma Inhaler Cracking my High Notes?

Dear Doctor Jahn,

I am fascinated by the amount of changes that happen in a young voice. I am 17 years old and am interested in a career in vocal performance. Recently I have been having trouble reaching my upper range without my voice cracking. These notes used to be extremely easy for me to reach. I haven't been vocalizing more than usual or changed anything about my lifestyle. The only changes are that I recently began taking an asthma controller medication (a steroid asthma spray) and have begun to learn to play the flute. Could either of these variables have created this change in my voice, or is the change just a common stage that my young voice is going through? I would really appreciate any insight that you could give me. - Hannah

Dear Hannah,

A number of issues come to mind. I am assuming at age 17 that you are fully grown, so your larynx would be at its adult dimensions. During puberty the larynx is unstable in terms of muscle control, which accounts for the pubertal wobble (called mutational falsetto) often heard in young teenage boys. It may be that your larynx, although anatomically adult in size, is still undergoing some muscular adjustments. A second issue has to do with what you are singing. If your voice has dropped during puberty (again, more of an issue in boys), you may not be as able to access those high notes without specific training.

Playing the flute is mostly a positive addition; exhaling against even slight resistance, focusing on the breath and connecting it to the sound are all good. I'm not sure whether you do thoracic or abdominal breathing for the flute, though, so consider whether that might be different than for singing.

Most important is the asthma spray; some of these (especially Advair) can cause hoarseness.

Steroid asthma sprays are known to be associated with a dry mouth and hoarseness. As with all steroid inhalers, there is also a risk of a yeast infection involving the hypopharynx and the larynx. If possible, you should stop your asthma spray (change to another effective medication) and have your larynx examined. If everything looks normal, return to your teacher to work on those high notes.

Symptom-Free Asthma Treatment: Myth or Reality?

Dear Doctor Jahn,

Are there any medications for asthma that you know of that do not affect the voice? Are there any oral treatments besides steroids in tablet form? Any advice you can give would be greatly appreciated! - Vicky

Dear Vicky,

ADVAIR, a frequently prescribed combination inhaler, does cause hoarseness. This is not usually an issue for non-singers, but is a big problem for singers, particularly higher voices. I wasn't aware of a similar problem with QVAR.

What can you do for your asthma? First, you need to figure out what kind of asthma you have. Some cases are triggered by allergy, infection, or exercise, and these may be controllable by managing the cause (controlling infections, shots, avoiding allergens, etc.). If your asthma is chronic, intrinsic, and requires ongoing treatment, consider the following options.

Singulair (generic name is monteleukast) is a non-steroidal tablet, and may be helpful for mild cases. I have seen no adverse reactions in singers, although it may not be strong enough for some cases. Inhalers such as albuterol do not affect the voice, but this is normally used only for acute flare-ups, not for long-term management. Serevent, one of the components in ADVAIR, may also be useful, and not as harmful to the singing voice.

You should also consider acupuncture. A number of acupuncture points can open up the lungs, decrease airway resistance, and reduce asthma.

Now, it may be that you absolutely have to use ADVAIR or QVAR.

Asthma can be a serious condition and its treatment may need to take precedence over other issues, but often, ADVAIR is used only because it is convenient—it is a combination of two drugs, easy to prescribe and easy to use. So, you may need to talk to another doctor who is more sympathetic to your singing and willing to spend the time to fine-tune your asthma management. I would generally not recommend chronic oral steroids, as these can have cumulative side effects that are potentially serious.

Seeking Moisture in a Dry Environment

Dear Doctor Jahn,

I've just moved to the desert and my singing voice is not the same. I'm assuming that my allergies are responsible for my constant mucus. When I hit a high note, it sounds awful. Furthermore, my left ear is always clogged up. Various remedies such as honey, water, Neti pot etc. do not seem to work – and I have a gig next week. Help! - Eve

Dear Eve,

You're most likely dealing with an overly dry climate. The vocal folds work best if the larynx is hydrated, both internally (the deeper tissues) and on the surface.

When the vocal folds vibrate, especially at higher frequencies, there needs to be a thin layer of fluid covering them. In effect, the contact between the two vocal folds is this cushion of thin fluid.

You can compare it to ice skating: the reason your skates glide easily on ice is because the blades actually slide on a thin layer of water caused by the heat generated by the weight of the skater. The actual sliding (or vocalizing) takes place on a fluid-covered surface. If the fluid is not there, then, in the case of the vocal folds, the voice sounds thin and rough. Trying to produce your normal sound only leads to excessive squeezing and further rubbing together of two dry vocal fold edges.

So you need to hydrate! Drinking water is helpful, especially if it's hot outside, and even more so if you exercise. I would suggest at least 60 ounces, spread over the course of the day. Keep your nose hydrated as well, with frequent sprays of saline. This is one situation where a small squeeze bottle of saline used frequently is actually more useful than a Neti pot.If you can obtain a saline nasal gel (marketed in the US under the brand name NaSal) this is even better, since the gel adheres to the nasal lining and keeps it moist longer.

Once your nose is wet, please remember to breathe through your nose (rather than your mouth) as much as you can; this humidifies the inhaled air and reduces laryngeal dryness.

Another issue may be allergies. The flora indigenous to deserts is usually not very allergenic, but we have imported a lot of non-indigenous plants to these areas (this is certainly true in areas of the US like Arizona), and with these plants come allergies. The dry desert wind carries pollen more easily and for greater distances.

Once the pollen is inhaled into a respiratory tract which is dry (i.e. under hydrated), it is more easily carried down to the larynx and the bronchial tubes. This, incidentally, may also account for your Eustachian tube blockage.

So, allergies are also a consideration. The dilemma here is, should you take a drying antihistamine to combat this? Look either to non-drying medications like Singulair (a leukotriene inhibitor, not an antihistamine), or natural anti-allergy remedies such as stinging nettle tea or capsules.

Longer-term allergy relief may be aided by eating local honey, which gently exposes your body to pollen - sort of like taking anti-allergy shots!

And finally, what is the elevation of this desert? Singing at higher altitudes actually adds to the misery, because the air is thinner and it is more difficult to support the voice. The body does get used to this thinner air over time, but initially you definitely need to use more muscle effort to get the voice out.

Seeking Solutions for Seasonal Voice Loss

Dear Doctor Jahn,

I sing a lot and take voice lessons and have zero problems – except that my voice gets raspy this time of year (autumn-winter). In the past, prednisone tablets have helped with this. Can I take these before the problem starts or do you have any other suggestions for my 'rasp'? - Barbara

Dear Barbara,

Autumn/winter raspiness may have several causes; let me propose a few, and you decide which one might fit your situation. Fall and winter allergies, usually to mould, often begin when the leaves fall and start to disintegrate. Increased rain and dampness can worsen this, especially if you spend time outdoors.

Spending time indoors can worsen dust allergies, so I would consider allergies as the first suspect. Speaking of indoor living, the air also becomes more dry once the heat is on. The lack of humidity can not only facilitate the free passage of dust, animal dander and pollen through the air, but can dry the vocal folds and make singing more difficult.

I would also look at your professional and social schedule: do you work more in the fall and winter, making greater demands on your voice? Are you singing more auditions, or playing more gigs around holiday time?

If your problem turns out to be allergies, I would take an antihistamine for one or two months. I have on occasion given patients with severe but limited (i.e. 1 or 2 months) allergies a shot of cortisone. While cortisone should not be used frivolously, it has the advantages of slow release. 40 mg of Depomedrol as an intramuscular injection can work for several weeks, with no dryness, and simplicity of administration – no need to take pills daily.

If your raspiness persists beyond the usual couple of months, have your larynx examined.
One concern is that you might develop some compensatory moves (pushing, straining, etc.) to overcome the hoarseness and, over time, the compensation might become a problem.

Am I Allergic to my New Neighborhood?

Dear Doctor Jahn,

Although I have never suffered from allergies before, since relocating I am fairly certain that I have allergies to the indigenous trees around here. I find that the walls of my throat and vocal folds are covered in a thin, clear, and quite pesky mucus. My teacher has suggested Claritin to help with the congestion that has also been a problem of late. I have heard that these newer anti-allergy medications are not as dehydrating and wondered what you thought about them. - Jimmy

Dear Jimmy,

My suggestion is first to be tested for allergies and find out whether you can avoid any of these allergens. Then, if you plan to stay in your current location, think about desensitization. There are several antihistamines available, including Claritin, Allegra, and Zyrtec, and each person reacts differently to these. You need to try them individually, preferably at a time when you don't need to sing, to see which one works the best for you. You should also consider Singulair (monteleukast), which controls leukotriene, an inflammatory substance like histamine. If this works for you, it is probably the best solution, since it is non-drying.

Stay well hydrated, including using saline spray to wash the pollen out of your nose. Finally, I recently heard from one of my patients that holistic MDs are using stinging nettle capsules (taken orally) to reduce allergies. This may be worth a try, since this would certainly be non-drying.

How Do I Maintain Vocal Health Around Wildfires?

Dear Doctor Jahn,

I'm a soprano living in an area affected by forest fires. I've been very lucky so far; my town is far enough away from the various fires that I haven't been evacuated, nor have any roads near my home been closed. However, the air quality has been bad. Because of the Angeles National Forest fire (the one closest to my house) the air has been thick and smoky.

I've followed the air quality warnings and stayed inside on the worst days. However, just from small excursions outside, my nostrils are burning and my throat is itchy. Besides the obvious (staying hydrated, following instructions. and staying inside on bad days) what else can singers do to ensure vocal health during the wildfires? Thanks so much for addressing this issue.

- Lettie

Dear Lettie,

You are doing the most important thing, which is staying indoors as much as you can. If you do need to go out, you could consider several preventive measures. First, spray your nose with saline before heading out. The best would be Ayr saline gel spray, an aqueous saline that is more viscous than just salt water and would protect your nasal lining better. If the air is particularly bad, consider wearing a mask—a cloth mask made damp with water would be the best way to catch any particulate matter in the air. On returning indoors, you should irrigate your nose with more saline, using a commercial nasal wash or a Neti pot.

Regarding your throat, try to breathe through your nose as much as possible, to filter the air that reaches your vocal cords. If you feel tightness or even wheezing, consider an asthma spray such as Albuterol. If you are prone to asthma, you may want to try Singulair tablets, although these take a bit longer to kick in than the inhalers.

And don't forget to drink lots of water. This is converted into a protective film of moisture that covers your respiratory lining.

12. Stage Fright and Vocal Health

My Stage Fright Causes Emergency Toilet Trips!

Dear Doctor Jahn,

I get so nervous before I sing that I literally feel like I'm going to poo my pants. Once I'm into the song this goes away but it's an excruciating and terribly uncomfortable feeling beforehand. What can I do to keep my stomach in check? - Bill

Dear Bill,

What you are describing, in your own charming way, is a case of stage fright. The need to evacuate your bowels and bladder in times of high anxiety is so common that during World War I, a favorite send-off to pilots who were heading out on a bombing mission was "Keep a tight asshole!" So, this is not new.

My suggestion, first, is to go to the bathroom before going on stage. If you do experience stage fright, you may wish to consider a low dose of Inderal (generic name is propranolol), a beta blocker which can reduce both your heart rate and your general anxiety level.

Other ways of managing stage fright abound, most importantly good preparation of your material, meditation, and visualization. But propranolol has stood the test of time, with the proviso that it might actually make you too calm, and take away some of the excitement of your performance.

So, good luck, and bombs away!

Will my Worrying Jinx my Vocal Health?

Dear Doctor Jahn,

Every time I have a gig, I worry that I will get a cold, or that my rehearsals leading up to the gig will wear out my voice for the gig. A friend told me that all my worrying could be causing some of my vocal problems! Could this be true? - Sienna

Dear Sienna,

You touched on two different issues (stress and excessive rehearsals), but they are related.

In general, worrying and anxiety are not helpful. While a certain amount of anticipatory excitement adds to the quality of your performance and makes it more "in the moment", excessive worry distracts and detracts from your work.

Not only does anxiety impede proper focus, it makes you sing with more tension.

From the laryngeal point of view, this causes excessive muscle contraction, decrease in the resonating spaces of the vocal tract, and a squeezed, harder and smaller voice. If this sort of singing is only occasional, you should not damage your larynx, although you may find you have a sore throat, sore neck and shoulder tension after performing.

When singing with tension becomes habitual, however, you may develop vocal fold nodules from overly squeezing the vocal folds together, causing trauma to the vibrating edges and callus formation. Once these nodules form, you enter a vicious cycle: to continue to approximate the folds for singing, you will have to squeeze harder and harder to get your voice. But increased squeezing, in turn, increases friction and trauma to the nodules, making them grow. Eventually, even with maximal "muscling", the voice will start to break up, you will lose notes off the top, and even your speaking voice might become husky.

There are many causes for phonating with excessive tension, but stress and worry are certainly right there near the top. On a more general level, stress can interfere with concentration, sleep, and even weaken your immune system, all of which can negatively impact on your performance.

Regarding excessive rehearsals: some of this behavior may also be driven by stress, and you need to figure out why you "need to rehearse" more than perhaps your vocal folds would like.

If the reason is to learn the music, by all means learn it! The best antidote to performance anxiety is to know your part cold. But learn the music (and words) in a way that is consistent with solid technique and smarter-not-harder practices as may be recommended by a good vocal coach – check out some of the excellent entries at VoiceCouncil.com from the many coaches who contribute regularly.

Analysis and understanding of WHAT you are trying to accomplish with your rehearsal is important; you only have a limited amount of miles on your vocal folds before the gig, so do not burn out with rehearsals.

Rehearsals are like Goldilocks' porridge: you shouldn't under-rehearse, but over-rehearsal is also bad: it not only tires you vocally, it also takes away some of the fun and spontaneity of the performance. While mindless repetition has a numbing, reassuring routine-like therapeutic effect on your brain, it comes with a price that your larynx may have to pay.

My Band Won't Change Song Keys – What Can I Do?

Dear Doctor Jahn,

My band likes to play our songs in the keys that they are used to, but often those keys are too high or too low for my voice, and require me to strain. What can I tell them to help them understand why singers need to sing songs that sit well in their range? - Mike

Dear Mike,

Your problem is one of communication with your band. Some instrumentalists simply don't appreciate what singers need to do. Specifically, they need to appreciate that singing in different parts of your vocal range is not a mechanical and arbitrary process like putting your finger on one key or fret versus another: you need to use different muscles in the throat, and you need to adjust your breathing and support.

So, while a song may be better for them in a certain key, either because it "sounds better" or is technically easier to play, you, as a singer, have specific anatomic and physiologic constraints attached to every sound you put out.

Rather than make this into a contest of wills, here is how you can all be on the same side of the argument. Let's assume that you all want the song to sound good. Explain to them that you have a specific range where you can sing really well, with good dynamics and physical comfort. Explain also that if you get outside of that range, your voice will be softer, less colorful and resonant, and generally less attractive.

You can add that singing at these extremes can also harm your voice, leading to vocal fatigue, voice damage, and eventually no lead singer. If they can appreciate this, they may be amenable to transposing the songs up our down a bit to accommodate your needs. They can always add dynamic and technical excitement in other ways, since all the notes are literally at their fingertips. But they are not at your fingertips! And your vocal folds, which are resilient but delicate, have certain physiologic limitations that need to be respected.

Could Stage Fright Medication Mess with my Voice?

Dear Doctor Jahn,

I am a singer who suffers from significant performance anxiety. My doctor has recommended the beta blocker Propranolol (Inderal) in doses of 5-20 mg before gigs. I'm concerned that that anti-anxiety drugs might affect voice quality. Could you give me any insight? - Gaz

Dear Gaz,

I would recommend that you try it. The main issue in our experience is that it takes some of the excitement out of performance, which in a performer with stage fright is exactly what you may want to do. Some singers feel that it flattens the performance, since they lose the "adrenaline rush" (and tachycardia) which may be important to the drama of the performance. It should have no significant effect otherwise (in terms of pitch or range). You should try it before a less important performance or audition and see how it affects you before using it for an important engagement.

My Stage Fright is Ruining my Career!

Dear Doctor Jahn,

I am a 30-year-old soprano with great promise. However, I am suffering from horrible performance anxiety. Please! I need your help. I am determined to fight this problem and empower myself, but I need your expert advice. Please tell me if you have any suggestions for coping with this.

(I sing beautifully when I know I have no important engagements—no vocal issues, no hoarseness—but once I have a competition or any important engagement my body and voice seem to have a mind of their own! I am stubborn and try to be brave, but lately I have been forced to cancel my participation in competitions because I wake up hoarse and unable to properly support my middle to high notes. It is horrific—to say the least—to be passionate about your art and when you have an opportunity to share it, get sick.) Please enlighten me with a way to effectively confront my problem! - Ivy

Dear Ivy,

First, you're not alone! Some of the greatest performers (Rachmaninoff comes to mind) had to be literally pushed on to the stage because of stage fright. You have several avenues to explore. One would be to talk to a psychologist who deals with performance anxiety.

Two, you could consider trying a beta blocker such as propranolol (Inderal) one hour before your performance. This does take some of the "edge" off your performance, but many musicians use this drug successfully.

Third, acupuncture, meditation, or visualization (not to clump all three together, because they are all very different) could be helpful.

Fourth, you may consider clinical hypnosis. A good hypnotist could help you to channel your excitement about performing into the performance itself, rather than into the negative feelings you develop.

Help Me Battle My Fear of Dentists!

Dear Doctor Jahn,

I have a very real phobia of dentists. I find the whole dental experience frightening because it is so closely linked to my voice. I am afraid of having my face, throat, or jaw permanently affected. I can't find a dentist who understands both the fear and my being a singer. I am wondering if you can give me some advice. - Peter

Dear Peter,

Many people have phobias about dentists—you're not alone! As far as specific issues related to singing, routine dentistry doesn't pose any risks to the voice. The one thing you should be aware of is that holding your mouth open for a prolonged period of time for some dental procedures can put a temporary strain on the temporomandibular joint. This can not only cause discomfort and temporary limitation on opening your mouth fully, but the increased muscle strain can reflexively elevate your larynx for a time. This, in turn, can affect your mix (passaggio). It's all temporary, though.

Dental issues are actually more significant for some wind players, such as flutists, where changing the orientation of the front teeth can affect the embouchure.

If your phobia is about dental surgery, you COULD consider taking a mild tranquilizer before the procedure. More natural methods such as meditation or listening to music can also allay the anxiety. The dental procedure itself should have no effect on your voice.

Could Braces Clamp Up my Voice?

Dear Doctor Jahn,

After years of dealing with uneven teeth, an orthodontist recommended wearing braces. My question is, how will wearing braces affect my singing? - Ronan

Dear Ronan,

I am happy to share some thoughts with you on this important topic, but you will also need to have a more informed discussion with your orthodontist, who is hopefully aware of, and sensitive to, your issues as a singer.

Braces nowadays are not as bulky and obtrusive as they used to be. Nonetheless, you are introducing a foreign body into the mouth. Even if this is small, it will likely have an effect on your articulation. If you like classic history, you may remember the Greek politician Demosthenes. The story goes that he had a bad stutter, which clearly got in the way of his speech. To cure himself, he went down to the seashore, and put a small pebble in his mouth. He then learned to speak again, this time with a pebble in his mouth, which slowed down his speech and put a brake on his stutter. The cure was a success, and Demosthenes became one of the great orators of his time. I tell you this story not only because I like it, but also to point out that any foreign body, even something a small as braces, may have some effect on your articulation. Sounds like "d" and "t" require you to put the tip of your tongue behind and against your upper incisors. You can of course sing with this, but it will be small but significant change.

The actual size of most braces is not big enough to significantly affect articulation, unless you need serious changes such as a palate expander, so I don't expect any change in resonance.

One other consideration is the discomfort associated with braces. Depending on how aggressively your orthodontist is moving those teeth around, you will have some discomfort which can translate into increased muscle tension in the jaw and the muscles positioning the larynx. This in turn can elevate the larynx, making the mix more difficult to smoothly negotiate. Of course, once you're past the initial straightening and wear your retainer only at night, this should no longer be a problem.

How Do You Sing with Hearing Aids?

Dear Doctor Jahn,

I have hearing aids, and am in the process of purchasing new ones, but just don't like how they feel when I sing. Do you have any advice for me? - Philippa

Dear Philippa,

You didn't tell me what the cause of your hearing loss is, how much hearing you have lost, and what kind of hearing aids you have been wearing. The fact that you have been a hearing aid user before suggests that the hearing loss is a significant nerve loss, but it gives you an advantage: your brain has become used to processing amplified sound. So, how can you make your new hearing aids comfortable for you, as a singer?

The mold, which fills and occludes the ear canal, is often a problem. It makes the sound unnatural and close. Further, since the shape of the ear canal changes as you open and close your mouth, it needs to be made expertly. It should be comfortable but snug so it doesn't pop out as you reach for those high notes.

One solution, depending on the severity of your hearing loss, is to consider an "open fit" hearing aid. This aid, for those with a mild or moderate high frequency loss, does not completely occlude the ear canal, and allows a blend of normal and amplified sound to reach the ear drum. It takes almost no time to get used to, and users find it comfortable and natural.

A more generic problem with most hearing aids is that they are digital rather than analog. This means that they heighten the contour between speech and background noise, making speech more crisp and understandable. The problem for you here is that we are dealing with music, not speech! Digital hearing aids do not faithfully track the gradual dynamic changes in music, making it sound unnatural and even choppy. In this regard, if you can possibly find an analog hearing aid, it would be better for music. Of course, another option is to leave your hearing aids out when performing, relying on ear-level monitors for the back-up band, and your proprioceptive cues (your body's sense of position) for the sounds you make.

And finally: the appearance. As hearing aid technology grows more miniaturized and sophisticated, hearing aids get smaller and less obtrusive. If appropriate for your degree of hearing loss, you may consider a CIC (completely-in the-ear) hearing aid, which truly cannot be seen. But even some behind-the-ear models (such as the open fit aids mentioned above) are so small that they would not present a cosmetic problem, unless you shave your head.

13. The Areas That Determine Your Sound

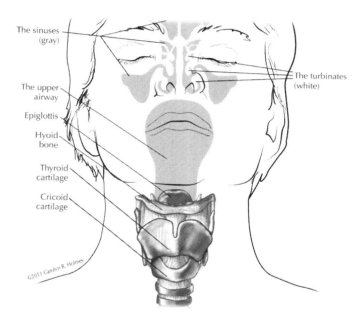

The sinuses (gray)

The turbinates (white)

The upper airway

Epiglottis

Hyoid bone

Thyroid cartilage

Cricoid cartilage

©2011 Carolyn R. Holmes

Figure 1
Frontal view illustrating the outer walls of the larynx and trachea
© Carolyn Holmes, M.S., C.M.I., F.A.M.I. Certified Medical Illustrator

The main structure of the laryngeal outer framework is the thyroid meaning "shield shaped" cartilage. A notch in the middle of the cartilage corresponds to the Adam's apple that you can feel in the middle of your neck.

The vocal folds attach to the inside of the thyroid Cartilage anteriorly, just below its middle. The thyroid cartilage is like a visor on a helmet. It hinges at the back on either side, next to the cricoid cartilage and swivels up and down as you go from chest voice into head voice. The laryngeal framework is attached above to the hyoid bone which, in turn, is attached to the base of the tongue. One of the tasks the trained singer needs to master is how to move these structures independently. This means, that you can drop the larynx without pushing the tongue back.

The gray areas above show the position of the pharynx, and then, around the eyes, the sinus cavities. These are involved in resonance, and amplify and color the voice. The sensation you feel when singing "in the mask" is simply vibration within the sinuses as sound waves reach this area.

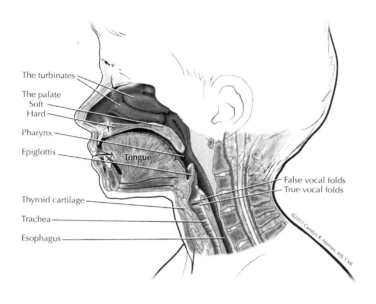

The turbinates
The palate
  Soft
  Hard
Pharynx
Epiglottis
Tongue
Thyroid cartilage
Trachea
Esophagus
False vocal folds
True vocal folds

©2011 Carolyn R Holmes, MS, CMI

Figure 2
Midline cross section of the upper airway
© Carolyn Holmes, M.S., C.M.I., F.A.M.I. Certified Medical Illustrator

Air is exhaled from the lungs and passes up the trachea to the vocal folds. The vocal folds vibrate and cause the air spaces above to begin to vibrate. Note the extensive resonating cavities above the larynx. These include the lower part of the throat (hypopharynx), as well as the back of the mouth (or in the front, within the oral cavity) Above the soft palate the nasopharynx and nasal cavities are also major resonating spaces for the voice.

Note the tongue which is a large mobile muscular structure. The shape and the position of the tongue determines whether the voice is in the back of the throat or forward. The size of the oropharynx space is determined by the position of the tongue and of the soft palate above. The size and configuration of this area changes moment to moment, and allows the singer to selectively amplify certain frequencies in the voice.

The anterior part of the mouth, including the tip of the tongue the lips and teeth, are the most important structures for articulation. When singing, the clarity of the one's words is largely determined by this area.

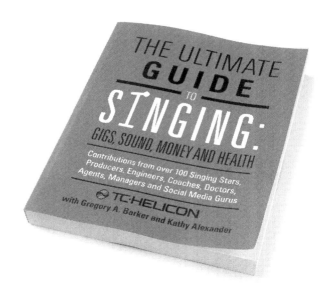

Also Available from TC-Helicon:
THE ULTIMATE GUIDE TO SINGING

Every aspect of singing and a singing life is addressed by leading experts from across the industry - from essential aspects of vocal technique and health to choosing a mic, running a sound system, mastering vocal effects, growing a fan base and achieving unforgettable performances and recordings.

Available from Amazon in both paperback and Kindle versions

Victoria, British Columbia, Canada, V8Z 3E9
info@TC-Helicon.com

TC-Helicon is an individual in TC Group, a collective of individuals passionate about sound.

Cover design by Jamie Drouin

66435515R00103

Made in the USA
Charleston, SC
18 January 2017